MUSIC LITERATURE OUTLINES

SERIES V

CHAMBER MUSIC FROM HAYDN TO RAVEL

by

HAROLD GLEASON

Sole Selling Agent   Levis Music Stores

Rochester 4, New York

PREFACE

The <u>Music Literature Outlines</u>, Series V, are intended to serve as a guide to the study of chamber music from Haydn to Ravel. Lists of books, periodicals, music and records will be found at the end of each <u>Outline</u>. When several recordings are listed for the same composition, they are in order of preference.

The study of the <u>Outlines</u> should be supplemented by performances of the music and by listening to recordings with scores. The student should purchase scores for his own use.

It should be pointed out that no attempt has been made to include all composers of chamber music, or all of the chamber music written by the composers represented. In general, the chamber music discussed is limited to works in the larger forms for ensembles of from three to six players, with emphasis on the string quartet. Sonatas for two instruments, and works for various wind and brass ensembles are not included, except in the Catalogue of Chamber Music given for each composer. Contemporary chamber music will be included in another series of <u>Outlines</u>.

The writer is indebted to Dr. Verne W. Thompson for help in the preparation of the <u>Outlines</u>.

September 1, 1955   Harold Gleason

CONTENTS

CHAMBER MUSIC FROM HAYDN TO RAVEL

ABBREVIATIONS

Periodicals

JAMS	Journal of the American Musicological Society
ML	Music and Letters
MM	Modern Music
MQ	Musical Quarterly
MR	Music Review
MT	Musical Times
MusAm	Musical America
MusCo	Musical Courier
MusOp	Musical Opinion

Records

All	Allegro
AS	L'Anthologie Sonore
BAM	Boite à Musique
Blue	Bluebeard
Cap	Capitol
CF	Cumberland Festival
CH(S)	Concert Hall (Society)
Clas	Classic
Col	Columbia
Dec	Decca
Gam	Gamut
Gram	Gramophone (HMV)
HS(Q)	Haydn Society (Quartets)
Lond	London
LP	Long playing
Lyr	Lyrichord
MC	Musicraft
Mer	Mercury
Ois	Oiseaux Lyre
Per	Period
Phil	Philharmonia
Poly	Polymusee
Rem	Remington
Sch	Schirmer
Str	Stradivari
Ura	Urania
Vic	Victor
West	Westminster

CHAMBER MUSIC FROM HAYDN TO RAVEL

OUTLINE I

INTRODUCTION

Music for Instrumental Ensembles before Haydn

I. Instrumental Ensembles

  A. Instrumental ensembles have been known since the late thirteenth century, when polyphonic dances and motets for two or three instruments were first written down.

  B. During the fourteenth century instruments were widely used, with voices and alone.

  C. In the fifteenth century, instrumental ensembles appeared in the Glogauer Liederbuch (c 1477-1488) and pieces were written by Ockeghem (c 1420-c 1495), Isaac (c 1450-1517), Hofhaimer (1459-1537), Obrecht (1450-1505), Josquin (c 1450-1521) and others.

  D. The sixteenth-century instrumental ensembles were also strongly influenced by the vocal style.

    1. Ricercari for instrumental ensembles (or keyboard) were written by many composers, including Buus (1547), Willaert (1549), A. Gabrieli (1571).

    2. Canzoni for instrumental ensembles were written by Maschera (1584), G. Gabrieli (1597) and others.

    3. Many dance pieces and a few fantasias were published in France and the Low Countries.

    4. Lassus published, in 1577, twelve pieces for two instruments. Eight ricercari are attributed to Palestrina.

    5. Fantasias in imitative style were written in England by Byrd, Gibbons and Weelkes.

  E. Seventeenth century

    1. At the beginning of the Baroque era the continuo became a part of almost all ensemble music.

    2. Canzoni, sometimes called "sonatas," were written by Viadana (1602), Merulo (1608), Hassler (1601), Schein (1609), Rossi (1608), Marini (1617), Frescobaldi (1628).

    3. The sonata da chiesa and sonata da camera developed from the multi-section canzone about 1665.

      a. The sonata da chiesa (church sonata), so-called because it was performed in church, became a standard four-movement form (Adagio-Allegro-Adagio-Allegro).

        1) The third and fourth movements were often dance-like, however.

      b. The sonata da camera (chamber sonata), so-called because it was not intended for church or operatic use, included dance movements.

      c. Compositions in these two forms were written by G. B. Vitali (1667), Arcangelo Corelli (1681-1712), Henry Purcell (1683, 1697), Johann Rosenmüller (1667).

  F. Eighteenth century

    1. The trio sonata (two violins and cello with basso continuo) developed c 1720 as a combination of elements found in both the sonata da chiesa and sonata da camera.

      a. It became the most important type of Baroque chamber music.

    2. Trio sonatas were written by Geminiani, Torelli, Caldara, Porpora, Dall'Abaco, Buxtehude, Handel, Bach (in the Musical Offering).

    3. The string quartet (two violins, viola, bass or cello) appeared about 1745 with the addition of the viola and the giving up of the basso continuo. After about 1750 the cello was used instead of the bass.

    4. The classical style began to develop about 1755.

      a. The Rococo composers (c 1725-1770) played an important part in the

1

        development of form and expressiveness.

    b.   D. Scarlatti, Pergolesi, Gluck, and the Sammartinis made innovations in the development of the sonata-form. Pergolesi and C. P. E. Bach used the fast-slow-fast sequence.

    c.   Johann Fasch and Telemann sometimes omitted the basso continuo and included the viola.

5.   The Viennese composers (c 1740-1765) Starzer, Monn, Wagenseil, included the minuet, omitted the continuo and developed the sonata-form.

6.   The Mannheim School (c 1743-1800), founded by Johann Stamitz, made important contributions to the classical style in the matter of orchestral discipline and the use of crescendo and the diminuendo, sudden fortes, homophonic writing, very fast allegros, "rocket" themes, tremolo, broken chords, and especially in the replacement of the basso continuo with written-out parts for instruments.

    a.   Composers were Richter, Holzbauer, Toëschi, Cannabich.

7.   Contemporaries of Haydn who were strongly influenced by the Mannheim composers include Johann Schobert (c 1720-1767) and Johann Christian Bach (1735-1782). Schobert increased the importance of the piano in chamber music and J.C. Bach wrote quintets (1776) for flute, oboe, violin, viola, cello which are complete without the continuo, although it is indicated.

OUTLINE II
FRANZ JOSEPH HAYDN (1732 - 1809)

I. Life

1732 Born in Rohrau-on-the-Leitha, Lower Austria, March 31, 1732. Left home at the age of five; received elementary instruction in Latin, singing, violin, harpsichord from a paternal cousin Johann Mathias Franck at Hainburg. Engaged by Georg Reutter (court composer and director of music) as chorister for St. Stephen's Cathedral in Vienna, and continued his education, mostly through his own efforts. Gave lessons, composed, practiced, played accompaniments. Studied by himself the sonatas and symphonies of C. P. E. Bach (1714-1788), Fux's (1660-1741) Gradus ad Parnassum and Mattheson's (1681-1764) Der vollkomene Capellmeister.

1755 Met Baron Karl Josef von Fürnberg of Weinzerl (near Vienna) through Metastasio the poet, and Porpora the singing teacher (1755). Was employed by von Fürnberg as violinist for about a year and composed his first quartets. Became composer and director of music to Count Ferdinand Maximilian von Morzin at Lukaveč, near Pilsen (1759). Married in 1760.

1761 Entered the service of the powerful and wealthy Esterházy (Eszterházy) family (Prince Paul Anton, 1761-62; Prince Nicholas, 1762-90) at Eisenstadt, Hungary. Here he provided two weekly operatic performances and two formal concerts. Publication of his music was begun by Artaria in Vienna (1769).

1790 Lived in Vienna after the death of Prince Nicholas (1790). Made two visits to London (1791-92; 1794-95) under the concert management of Johann Salomon; wrote and conducted the twelve "Salomon" Symphonies; received the honorary Mus. Doc. degree from Oxford.

1798 Composed songs, quartets, two oratorios (The Creation, 1798; The Seasons, 1801) in his last years. Dictated to Elssler, his copyist and secretary, a "catalogue of those compositions which I recall offhand having composed from my 18th to my 73rd year." Composed the Austrian national anthem, "The Emperor's Hymn" (1797).

1809 Died in Vienna on May 31 at the age of 77. Buried in the Hundsturm churchyard and later (1820) reinterred at Eisenstadt.

II. Catalogue of Chamber Music

 A. String Instruments
  1. Quartets
   a. 84 for 2 violins, viola, cello (1755-1809)
    1) This number includes the "Interludes to the Seven Last Words, Op. 51," which Haydn arranged for string quartet, and the "Lost Heir," in E-flat (No. 0), recently discovered. Included also is an incomplete work (Op. 103) in B-flat.
   b. 1 for lute, violin, viola, cello, in D.
  2. Duos
   a. 3 for 2 violins
   b. 1 for barytons, in G (after 1762)
   c. 1 for violin, cello in D (before 1783)
   d. 6 Sonatas for violin, viola (C, A, E-flat, F, D, B-flat) (after 1770)
   e. 1 for 2 lutes

   3. Trios.
      a. 18 for 2 violins, cello (harpsichord ad lib.) (E, F, D, E-flat, A,
         B, F, c, E, D, C, E-flat, B-flat, E, G, D, D, G) (c 1760).
      b. 12 Divertimenti for 2 barytons, bass (cello) (after 1762).
      c. 125 for baryton, viola, cello (1762-75).
         1) The baryton was a gamba-like instrument with six gut strings and
            twelve sympathetic strings. The sympathetic strings, usually
            metallic, were strung underneath the carved-out fingerboard.
            These could be plucked by the left thumb, while the gut strings
            over the fingerboard were bowed.
      d. 1 Cassation for lute, violin, cello, in C.
         1) Cassations designed for outdoor performance; especially adapted
            to music for weddings, festivals, birthdays, etc. Practically
            identical in form with Divertimenti and Serenades.
      e. 1 Divertimento for viola d'amore, violin, cello, in E-flat (also in
         D).
   4. Quintets
      a. 1 for 2 violins, 2 cellos, bass (flute ad lib.), in G (1754).
   5. Sextets
      a. "Echo" for 4 violins, 2 cellos (or piano, 2 violins, cello), to be
         performed in 2 separate rooms (before 1767).
B. String with Other Instruments
   1. 8 Sonatas for violin, piano (harpsichord).
      a. G (before 1790).
      b. D (1773) from Piano Sonata 22.
      c. E-flat (1773) from Piano Sonata.
      d. A (1773) from Piano Sonata 24.
      e. G, Op. 70 (1794). Only composition composed originally in this
         form, others taken from piano sonatas, divertimenti, string
         quartet.
      f. C (before 1767). Transcription of parts of a Divertimento for
         flute, oboe, 2 violins, cello, bass.
      g. F (1799). Transcription of parts of String Quartet Op. 77, No. 2
         (Minuet omitted).
      h. G (1799). Transcription of parts of String Quartet Op. 77, No. 1
         (Minuet omitted).
   2. Trios
      a. 31 for piano, violin, cello (c 1770-96).
         1) As numbered in Breitkopf & Härtel ed.: G, f#, C, E, E-flat, D,
            A, C, A, e, E-flat, E-flat, B-flat, g, E-flat, g, E-flat, C, d,
            E-flat, D, B-flat, F, A-flat, F, C, F, G, D, G.
      b. 3 for piano, flute, bass.
      c. 4 for 2 flutes, cello (flute, violin, cello?) (C, G, G, G) (1794).
      d. 2 for flute, violin, bass (1794?).
      e. 1 Divertimento for horn, violin, cello, in E-flat (1767).
      f. 1 for corno da caccia, violin, cello (1794?).
      g. 1 Sonata for harpsichord, flute, bass (1794).
      h. 3 for 3 flutes.
      i. 1 Trio sonata (Divertimento) for piano, 2 violins, in B-flat.
   3. Quartets
      a. 6 for flute, violin, viola, cello (1770).
      b. 1 Divertimento for oboe, violin, viola da gamba, bass, in B-flat
         (1767).
      c. 1 for harpsichord, 2 violins, baryton in F (before 1762); published
         also as String Trio No. 25.
   4. Sextets
      a. 1 for flute, oboe, bassoon, violin, cello, bass, in E-flat (1782).
      b. 1 Divertimento for flute, oboe, 2 violins, cello, bass, in C (6th
         Sonata for violin, piano) (before 1767).
      c. 1 Cassation for flute, oboe, 2 violins, cello, bass, in G (1768).
   5. Octets
      a. 1 for 2 horns, 2 English horns, 2 violins, 2 basses (1760).

  b. 1 for 2 oboes, 2 clarinets, 2 bassoons, 2 horns, in F (1760).
  c. 6 Scherzandi for 2 horns, 2 oboes, flute, 2 violins, bass (F, C, D,
    G, E, A) (before 1757).
  d. 1 Divertimento for 2 English horns, 2 bassoons, 2 violins, 2 horns,
    in F (1760).
  e. 6 Divertimenti for flute, 2 horns, 2 violins, viola, cello, bass
    (G, A, G, D, G, D) (before 1781). All were previously baryton
    compositions, except No. 1.
  f. 6 Feld Partiten for 2 oboes, 2 horns, 3 bassoons, serpent (or for 2
    oboes, 2 clarinets, 2 horns, 2 bassoons) (c 1780). Feld Partita in
    D-flat, with the "Chorale At. Antoni" used by Brahms in Op. 56.
 6. Nonets
  a. 1 for 2 oboes, 2 horns, 2 violins, viola, cello, bass (before 1757).
  b. 1 Cassation for 2 oboes, 2 horns, 2 violins, 2 cellos, bass, in G
    (before 1764).
  c. 7 Notturnos for 2 lyra organizata, 2 clarinets, 2 horns, 2 violas,
    bass (C, F, G, F, C, G, D) (1790).
   1) Lyra organizata was a type of hurdy-gurdy, sometimes with small
     organ pipes. A typical hurdy-gurdy had a wheel handle and key-
     board mounted on a small viol. Usually three or four bass
     strings which sounded in drone harmony continuously; two melody
     strings (tuned in unison) stopped by tangents operated by keys.

III. Chamber Music

 A. Haydn was the first great master of the new instrumental style which cul-
  minated in the works of Beethoven. He refined and clarified the forms
  and achievements of his predecessors and effected the transition from the
  aesthetic system of Bach to that of the classicists in an orderly progress
  of works. He had original and inexhaustible melodic gifts and creative
  resources and was a master of gayety, humor, tenderness and passion.
  1. Problems of instrumentation, both in chamber music and the orchestra,
   many of which lay in the distribution of the continuo-function among
   all the instruments, were largely unresolved when Haydn began to
   compose. Among the problems were the special technique of the various
   instruments and the contrasting and blending of tones of those instruments into the harmonic structure.
  2. A unique feature of Haydn's chamber music is his scoring of the same
   music for different instruments. His early chamber music often belongs
   more to orchestral literature than to chamber literature. In this
   category are the Divertimenti, Cassations, Nocturnes, Scherzi, and some
   smaller works. On the other hand, the violin and clavier sonatas as
   well as the clavier trios belong more to the field of piano literature.
 B. Sonata-form (sonata-allegro; first-movement form)
  1. The form usually used for the first, and sometimes for other movements
   of a quartet, symphony, concerto, or sonata.
   a. The sonata-form has been in continual use since the time of Haydn,
    although in the twentieth century it has been subjected to many
    modifications.
  2. The sonata-form emerged from the cyclic binary form, :A::BA:,
   with the use of two themes (often contrasting) in the first "A" section.
   The repeats in the second half were later omitted.
  3. Final development of sonata-form (A A B A).
   a. Exposition: Theme (group) I in tonic, Theme (group) II in dominant.
    1) If Theme I is in minor, Theme II will be in the relative major
     (Haydn and Mozart) or dominant minor.
    2) Bridge passages or transitions connect the themes.
    3) Closing theme at the end of Theme II is in the dominant.
     a) Later (Brahms) this theme often becomes Theme III.
     b) Repetition of the Exposition was usual until the time of
      Brahms.

       b. <u>Development</u> (fantasia). Function is to develop the material of the
         Exposition in various ways.
         1) Fragmentation of themes.
         2) Rapid harmonic modulations.
         3) Use of contrapuntal devices.
         4) Occasional use of new themes.
       c. <u>Recapitulation</u>
         1) Material of Exposition restated more or less exactly. Bridge
         passages are usually modified.
         2) Theme (group) I in tonic.
         3) Theme (group) II in tonic.
       d. <u>Coda</u> is usually short until the time of Beethoven.

C. The String Quartet
    1. Haydn was vitally interested in the string quartet and made a special
      contribution to the form. He composed quartets for over fifty years,
      experimenting with contrapuntal forms, key relationships, and thematic
      development. Each quartet has a character of its own, and almost all
      show his steady musical progress.
    2. Major keys predominate; themes are usually diatonic (chromatic lines
      between 1785-90); variations are usually of the cantus <u>firmus</u> type;
      there is considerable doubling in thirds and sixths; phrases are often
      of uneven length (5 or 7 meas.).
    3. Chromatic lines appear in Op. 9, Nos. 1, 6; Op. 17, Nos. 2, 3, 6;
      Op. 20, Nos. 2, 4; Op. 33, Nos. 1, 3, 4; Op. 42. Principal use of
      chromatic lines is in Op. 50, 54, 55, 64. Some use in the later
      quartets, Op. 71, No. 3; Op. 74, No. 1; Op. 77.
    4. Forms
      a. The sonata-form became the standard form for the first movement, and
        the rondo, sonata-rondo, or sonata-form for the last movement.
      b. Variations are used for first movements in Op. 2, No. 6; Op. 3, No.
        2; Op. 9, No. 5; Op. 17, No. 3; second movement in Op. 20, No. 4.
      c. Fugues are used for last movements in Op. 20, Nos. 2, 5, 6; Op. 50,
        No. 4.
      d. Minuets are used for both the second and fourth movements of Op. 1
        and 2. Op. 1, No. 5 (a symphony) has only three movements (F-S-F).
        Op. 3, No. 4 has two movements (F-SFSF).
        1) The minuet is used for the second movement in Op. 3, Nos. 1, 2;
          Op. 9; Op. 17; Op. 20, Nos. 1, 3, 5; Op. 42; Op. 64, Nos. 1, 4;
          Op. 77, No. 2; Op. 103 (incomplete).
        2) Third movement in Op. 3, Nos. 3, 5, 6; Op. 20, Nos. 2, 4, 6; Op.
          64, Nos. 1, 4.
      e. Scherzi are used for second movements in Op. 33, Nos. 1, 2, 3, 4;
        third movements in Nos. 5, 6. A Fantasia (Adagio) is the second
        movement in Op. 76, No. 6.

D. Summary of Quartets
    1. Op. 1, 2 (1755), which include two minuets, were first known as di-
      vertimenti. Homophonic style, first violin prominent, two-part form
      form predominates.
      a. Op. 3 (<u>c</u> 1755-65) established the four-movement form and a rudiment-
        ary sonata-form
    2. Op. 9 (<u>c</u> 1769) shows for the first time, according to the composer, his
      real style.
    3. Op. 17 (1771) marks a second advance in technique and expression.
    4. Op. 20 (1772) reveals marked progress toward equality in the use of all
      four instruments, especially the cello, and the first use of fugue.
    5. Op. 33 (1781) was "written in an entirely new manner" in which the use
      of thematic fragmentation and real thematic development are character-
      istic.
    6. Op. 50, 51, 54, 55, 64 (1785-90) were written during the years of
      Mozart's strongest influence upon Haydn. This influence is seen in

many ways, including the use of chromatic lines, expansion of thematic material and expressive resourcefulness.

7. Op. 71, 74, 76, 77 (1791-99) were concerned principally with considerations of expressiveness and the broadening of internal dimen-
sions rather than in any basic alterations in design or procedure.

IV. String Quartets
    A. Op. 1 (c 1755): 6 quartets in B-flat ("La Chasse"), E-flat, D, G, B-flat
        (originally Haydn's first symphony), C.
    B. Op. 2 (1755): 6 quartets in A, E, E-flat, F, D, B-flat.
        1. Op. 1 and 2 were written while Haydn was in the employ of von Fürn-
            berg (1755-56). He was influenced primarily by works of Viennese
            pre-classicists: George Reutter, Jr., George C. Wagenseil, Mathias
            G. Monn.
        2. Most of the quartets in Op. 1 and Op. 2 were known as "Divertimenti"
            for two violins, viola, and basso (cello or bass).
            a. Op. 2, Nos. 3 and 5, were originally sextets with two horns (arr.
                by Haydn for string quartet).
        3. Op. 1 and Op. 2 have five movements, which include two minuets (ex-
            cept Op. 1, No. 5). Usual order: Fast-Minuet-Slow-Minuet-Fast.
        4. The two-part forms used at first, gradually show some evidences of
            feeling for sonata-form.
            a. Second subject in the dominant key, but often related to the
                first subject.
            b. Transitions between the second subject and the recapitulation be-
                came longer, suggesting a development section.
        5. Sequences, repetition, prominent first and second violins, doubling
            of the viola and cello (melodically or rhythmically), diatonic
            melodies, homophonic texture, irregular phrase lengths are a part of
            the style of the early quartets.
    C. Op. 3 (c 1755-65): 6 quartets in E, C ("Fantasia con Variazioni"), G
        (Minuet called "Bagpipe"), B-flat, F ("Serenade").
        1. Four movements become the standard form, with some exceptions.
            a. Minuet is used second in Nos. 1 and 2, third in Nos. 3, 5, 6;
                different tempos are used for the first and final movements (No.
                2, 1st mvt., is a theme and five variations).
            b. More ornamentation at cadence points; accompanying parts are given
                more independence; first and last movements are still very fast.
        2. Op. 3, No. 5 (F). Presto-Andante cantabile-Menuetto-Scherzando.
            a. Four movements in the new order: Fast-Slow-Minuet-Fast. First
                movement shows first real use of the sonata-form; second theme is
                in direct contrast to the principal theme; development section
                uses some unrelated keys; transitions, codettas, closing themes
                are longer and more important.
            b. First movement (Presto).
                1) Exposition (meas. 1-90): first theme (meas. 1-16); codetta
                    (meas. 17-23); transition (meas. 24-41); second theme (meas.
                    41-65); closing group (meas. 66-83); codetta (meas. 84-90).
                2) Development (meas. 91-138): part of first theme (meas. 91-98);
                    melodic embellishment of principal theme in d (meas. 99-106);
                    development of fragment of theme from measure 24 in A, D, G,
                    g, f, using imitation (meas. 106-113).
                3) Recapitulation (meas. 138-224): first theme slightly altered
                    melodically (meas. 138-153); codetta altered harmonically
                    (meas. 154-157); transition harmonically altered (meas. 158-
                    175); second theme in tonic, harmonically and melodically al-
                    tered (meas. 176-199); closing group melodically altered (meas.
                    200-217); codetta as in measures 84-90 (meas. 218-224).
            c. The famous "Serenade" has a typical song-like melody in the first
                violin with a pizzicato chordal accompaniment.

      d. Last movement (Scherzando).
         1) Sonata-form. Exposition: first theme (meas. 1-8); bridge (meas. 8); second theme (meas. 20); Development (meas. 45-61); Recapitulation (meas. 61).

V. String Quartets, Op. 9, 17, 20 (1769-1772)
  A. Op. 9 (c 1769): 6 quartets in C, E-flat, G, d, B-flat, A.
    1. Between Op. 3 and Op. 9, Haydn wrote forty symphonies. Haydn wished to discard the first eighteen quartets and begin with Op. 9, in which he felt his real style manifested itself. Op. 9 shows marked progress in quartet writing. The first violin part is still brilliant; themes are more imaginative, shorter, and better suited to development; longer development sections.
    2. First movement is a moderate Allegro (except No. 5, a Theme and four Variations); the second a Minuet; the third a slow movement; the last movement retains its usual lively, humorous character.
    3. Melodic lines are more elaborate, but still primarily diatonic; cadences still sometimes ornamented; retardation of leading-tone to tonic a common feature.
    4. No. 2 (E-flat) has an eight-measure recitative introduction to the slow movement. No. 4 (d) uses dramatic pauses, syncopation, chromaticism, scherzo-like finale. No. 5 (1st mvt.) has a Theme and Variations in a new form built on alternating themes. No. 6 makes some use of chromatic lines.
  B. Op. 17 (1771): 6 quartets in E, F, E-flat, c, G, D.
    1. New features appear; style becomes richer, more profound and expressive in the slow movements.
      a. Fast movements have more virtuoso-like first violin parts (double stops, arpeggios, crossing of strings, use of highest register).
      b. Material is more evenly divided among the instruments; more thematic material is given to the second violin, viola and cello; viola and cello achieve more independence.
    2. Minuet the second movement in all quartets of Op. 17; Theme and Variations is used for first movement of No. 3. Influence of Croatian folk songs is seen in No. 6.
  C. Op. 20 (c 1772): 6 quartets in E-flat, C, g, D, f, A.
    1. Called "Sun Quartets," from symbol of rising sun printed on an early edition. The names which are associated with the quartets were not given to them by Haydn. No one quartet is typical of the set; individual differences between quartets are more marked than similarities.
    2. Form of the quartet, except for the Minuet, is finally established. Minuet is used for second movement in Nos. 1, 3, 5; third movement in Nos. 2, 4, 6.
      a. Variation form is used for second movement (No. 4).
      b. Final movements in Nos. 2, 5, 6 are 4-voice fugues (first use in quartets), labelled two, three, or four subjects (Soggetti), depending on how many counter-melodies accompany the principal subject throughout the fugue.
      c. Style galant is less in evidence; new regard for tone color and melodic possibilities of the scale. True four-voice texture is gradually appearing as cello becomes more important; fugal writing the logical outcome.
    3. No. 2 (C). Moderato-Adagio-Menuetto-Allegro.
      a. First movement shows a fully developed sonata-form; begins with a cello solo (first time the violin has not dominated); imitation used between outer voices (meas. 48-60).
      b. Adagio opens with unison recitative suggestive of Beethoven, followed by a solo cadenza for violin.
      c. Minuet uses "drone" figures.
      d. Fourth movement a "Fuga a IV Soggetti."

    4. No. 5 (f). Allegro moderato-Menuetto-Adagio-Finale.
       a. First movement has first and second endings for the development and recapitulation; movement concludes with an extended coda.
       b. Adagio has striking chain of dissonances (section marked "per figuram retardationis") caused by first violin being slightly behind the change of chord.
       c. Fugal finale, "a due Soggetti," is based on a theme similar to "And With His Stripes," from Handel's <u>Messiah</u>; stretto near the end of fugue is separated by a pause on the dominant.

VI. String Quartets, Op. 33, 42 (1781-1783)
  A. Op. 33 (1781): 6 quartets in b (D), E-flat ("The Joke"), C ("The Bird"), B-flat, G, D. Dedicated to Grand Duke Paul of Russia.
    1. "Composed in a new and special manner" (Haydn) in which homophonic and polyphonic elements are satisfactorily combined. These quartets represent the first real thematic development; based on breaking up of phrases and contrapuntal development of the fragments. Called "Russian" or, because of a picture on the title page, "Jungfern" Quartets; also known as "Gli Scherzi," as each quartet has a movement marked "Scherzo" in place of the usual Minuet.
       a. First time "Scherzo" appears in Haydn's chamber music; term was not used after Op. 33, but the characteristics persisted in later Minuets.
    2. Thematic material is still more evenly divided among the instruments; initial melody sometimes given to another instrument besides the first violin (examples: No. 6, Andante, the second violin; No. 2, Largo, a duet for viola and cello).
       a. Melodies diatonic, but with occasional chromatic lines (No. 1, Andante, sixth measure before the end; Nos. 3, 4).
    3. Major mode most used, with modulations to closely related keys.
       a. "False starts," pizzicato, use of half-cadence, and folk-like melodies give indication of Haydn's humor.
       b. Minuets are lighter and more Mozart-like, often with scherzo character.
       c. Fewer ornaments in the slow movements than in earlier periods, showing a change from Rococo to Classic style.
       d. Rondo form is used for the last movements, except in Nos. 1 and 5. Final movement of No. 6 consists of variations on two themes, one major and one minor (characteristic of Haydn).
    4. No. 2 (E-flat) is called "The Joke" because of humorous and unexpected ending of the Presto (finale); theme of the Coda is a modified statement of the first theme; cadence in measure 166 like end of first section (meas. 8); unexpected final cadence like measures 2-3.
       a. This quartet is typical of this period, with emphasis on thematic and rhythmic development and better balance of parts.
       b. Development section of the first movement uses mostly motives from the first theme; modulations to G-flat, D-flat (meas. 46).
    5. No. 3 (C) was called "The Bird" because of grace notes used and developed in the first and final movements, and the "bird-like" violin duet in the scherzando trio. There is some influence of Croatian folk songs.
  B. Op. 42 (1768 or 1783 or 1785): one quartet in d.
    1. Contains devices and elements seemingly suggesting both earlier and later styles, such as the dramatic development in the first movement, contrapuntal devices in the finale and pianissimo endings.
    2. First movement is slow; second movement a Minuet; third movement marked "Adagio e cantabile," shows unique lyric writing with a long, singing melody; dinale, marked "Presto," is written in imitative style; second violin begins the theme.

VII. String Quartets, Op. 50, 51, 54, 55, 64 (1785-1790)

    A. Op. 50 (<u>c</u> 1784): 6 quartets in B-flat, C, E-flat, f-sharp, F (with Adagio, "The Dream"), D ("The Frog").
        1. Dedicated to Frederick William II, king of Prussia, a capable cellist; emphasis is on cello part; more difficult technically, richer, more lyrical and dramatic than in earlier quartets.
           a. First and second "themes" now often consist of several phrases, usually called "first group" and "second group."
           b. Thematic development appears in recapitulations as well as in development sections.
           c. Marked use of chromatic lines, which begins in these quartets, shows the influence of Mozart.
        2. Minuet is consistently used again, this time (and for most of the remaining quartets) as the third movement.
           a. Finales are all sonata-form except No. 4, which is a fugue (last of the entirely fugal movements).
           b. Fully developed and brilliant codas in place of the recapitulation (exact return of first and second theme groups no longer followed).
        3. No. 4 (f-sharp) has a change of mode between first and second subjects of first movement.
           a. Andante alternates between major and minor modes and combines rondo-like features with theme and variations.
           b. Key of six sharps used for first time (in first movement and Minuet).
           c. Fourth movement is a fugue.
        4. No. 5 (F) contains a slow movement known as "The Dream," from elaborate solo passages for the violin.
           a. Third movement (Minuet and Trio) uses the same grace-note motif.
        5. No. 6 (D) is called "The Frog" because of gay "croaking" sounds in the Finale, made by rapid alternation of the same note on two neighboring strings (bariolage).
           a. Unusual expansion of the Minuet trio gives new treatment of material instead of conventional re-use of a new theme.

    D. Op. 51 (arr. 1787-94): 7 quartets in d-B-flat (Introduction and Largo), c-C, E, f, A, g-G, E-flat, c (Largo with Presto "Earthquake")
        1. Arranged by Haydn from the Good Friday music composed for Cadiz Cathedral in 1785 under the title of <u>Seven Last Words of Christ</u>.
           a. The original music was composed for orchestra, the form consisting of an Adagio introduction, seven slow movements in free sonata-form, and a Finale.
           b. Vocal parts and a sacred text were added by Friebert in 1792 and later revised by Haydn.

    E. Op. 54 (1788-90): 3 quartets in G, C, E
        1. First movement in sonata-form; slow second movement is in the key of the subdominant or parallel mode; Minuet is in original key; Presto finale is in original key.
        2. Writing harmonic rather than contrapuntal, with thematic material well divided among the four instruments. The music in general shows even greater melodic charm than in earlier works. Cadential dissonances are used more sparingly; some use of chromatic lines, but not in main theme.
        3. No. 1 (G) has modulations to unusual keys (B-flat, D-flat, E-flat, G-flat) in the second movement (Allegretto in C).
        4. No. 2 (C) has large and symphonic first movement; dissonances built on a fourth (Minuet); crossing of parts (cello above violins and viola) in Adagio introduction to final Presto.

    F. Op. 55 (1788-90): 3 quartets in A, f ("The Razor"), B-flat. Dedicated to Johann Tost.
        1. From this point on, each quartet is an unique and individual masterpiece. Minuet still consistently used as third movement; examples of

chromaticism in each quartet in Op. 55.
  2. No. 1 (A) has an Adagio in rondo form; employs extreme upper range of
      the violin in the Minuet; concludes with a Finale which begins as a
      rondo and ends as a double fugue.
      a. Some influence of Austrian and Hungarian folk melodies.
  3. No. 2 (f) is known as "The Razor" Quartet because of an exchange (a
      quartet for a good razor) bargained with a friend.
      a. The first movement is a set of variations in slow time, alternat-
          ing major and minor.
G. Op. 64 (1790): 6 quartets in C, b, B-flat, G, D ("The Lark"), E-flat.
    Dedicated to Johann Tost.
  1. Forms are much the same as those already established; slow movement
      follows Minuet in Nos. 1 and 4; simple rondo form is replaced in the
      finales with well developed sonata-rondos.
  2. New key relationships and keys appear in these and the following
      groups of quartets. Chromatic lines in Nos. 2, 4, 5, 6.
  3. No. 5 (D) is called "The Lark" because of the upward-soaring, high
      melody in the first violin part. Minuet has interesting canonic writ-
      ing. Finale is a perpetuum mobile with a fugato at the beginning of
      the development section.
  4. No. 6 (E-flat). Last quartet of the Esterházy period, and a quartet
      of exceptional workmanship. More attention is given to the viola than
      before (development section of the first movement). Final Presto is
      built on a folk-like theme.

VIII. String Quartets, Op. 71, 74, 76, 77, 103 (unfinished) (1791-1803)
  A. These quartets show perfect balance between homophonic and polyphonic
      styles, combined with great freedom of form. Introductions, effective
      slow movements, and marked dynamic effects are characteristics. From
      Op. 71 on, the quartets are all on a symphonic scale.
  B. Op. 71 (1791-93): 3 quartets in B-flat, D, E-flat. Dedicated to Count
      Apponyi.
    1. From Op. 71 on, the use of chromaticism is rare. Third movements are
        always in Minuet form. Slow movement of No. 3 is in rondo-variation
        form. First movements have introductions (a feature of Haydn's sym-
        phony form), consisting of chords only in Nos. 1 and 3, and a four-
        measure Adagio in No. 2. Fugato is used at the beginning of the de-
        velopment section in the last movement of No. 1.
    2. Interesting crossing of the cello and viola parts in No. 3 (develop-
        ment section of first movement) produces second-inversion chords (meas.
        129-132). Slow movement, in rondo-variation form, shows a new use of
        tone color. A little use of chromaticism.
  C. Op. 74 (1793-94): 3 quartets in C, F, g ("The Rider"). Dedicated to
      Count Apponyi.
    1. Tendencies toward Romanticism and freedom in key relationships are
        characteristics of this group. Remote keys are used in the trios of
        Minuets, a characteristic of quartets from Op. 74 on.
    2. No. 1 (C): first movement opens with a two-chord introduction; fugato
        at beginning of development section. First and final movements con-
        tain a development in the recapitulation. Trio of the Minuet (C)
        goes to the remote key of A-flat without modulation.
    3. No. 2 (F): second movement (Andante grazioso) is composed of theme and
        three florid variations; second violin is prominent in second varia-
        tion. Minuet shows a sharp key contrast (F to D-flat in Trio). In-
        fluence of Croatian folk songs.
    4. No. 3 is called "The Rider" from galloping figure that introduces the
        first movement; fugato at the beginning of the development section.
        The second movement (Largo assai) in E, has a short section in e. The
        brilliant Finale uses Hungarian and Austrian folk tunes.
  E. Op. 76 (1797-98): 6 quartets in G, d ("Quinten"), C ("Emperor"), B-flat

("Sunrise"), D, E-flat (with the "fantasia")

1. These quartets reveal maturity of style and are direct, condensed, and intense in personal expression. Tempos are faster; Minuets become more like scherzi. Only two quartets and part of a third were composed after this opus.

2. An unusual feature is found in the Finales of Nos. 1 and 3 which begin in the parallel minor key. Fugal entries are found in No. 1 (first movement) and No. 6 (coda of first movement and "alternative" of Minuet).

3. No. 2 (d) is called the "Quinten" because of descending fifths in the opening theme. "Hexen ('Witches') Minuet" is a two-part canon between the violins in octaves and the viola and cello in octaves.

4. No. 3 (C)("Emperor" or "Kaiser") includes the famous variations on "God Save our Emperor" which later became the Austrian National Anthem. Haydn set the words to music in 1797 during the war between Austria and France.

   a. Dotted-note rhythm (much used by Beethoven) of the first movement is found in the Minuet in reverse order. The four variations (second movement) use the theme without change, in the second violin, cello, viola, first violin. The Presto finale in c minor is based on a triplet figure with many imitations and overlappings; slow sections serve to intensify the drive of the movement.

   b. First movement (Allegro).

     1) Exposition (meas. 1-44): 1st theme divided into 3 motives (meas. 1, 2, 3) used in various ways; scale-line motive in dotted-note rhythm combined with 1st motive of 1st theme (meas. 5-7); bridge passage (meas. 8-12) over tonic and dominant pedal closes on G (meas. 12); 1st and 3rd motives in imitation (meas. 13-17); transitory passages over a pedal point on D lead to a V_7 chord in G (meas. 22), followed by a thematically important passage (meas. 23-25) leading to the 2nd theme. 2nd theme (meas. 26-27) related to motive 2 of 1st theme (meas. 2); transitory passage (meas. 28) modulates to E-flat (meas. 31); motive 1 of 1st theme used in canonic imitation (meas. 33); 2nd theme introduced in dominant key (G) and exposition concludes in that key with first and second endings.

     2) Development (meas. 45-78): material from 1st theme, combined with dotted-note rhythm (meas. 45-48); transition using first 2 motives of 1st theme (meas. 49-51); 2nd motive of 1st theme (meas. 52-56); material from meas. 23-25 (meas. 57-64) with cadence in E (meas. 65); 1st theme and dotted-note rhythm with pedal point in open 5ths (meas. 65-75); modulation to C through c over a pedal point on E (meas. 75-78).

     3) Recapitulation (meas. 79-121): repetition of material of Exposition (meas. 79-87); transitory passage in G (meas. 90-94) leading to a V_7 chord in C (meas. 94); codetta in C (meas. 95-97); 2nd theme in tonic (meas. 98).

     4) Coda (meas. 105-121) uses 2-note motive from 1st theme (meas. 105-107); modulating passage leads to statement of 2nd theme in tonic. Development, Recapitulation and Coda are repeated.

5. No. 5 (D) includes the famous Largo in F-sharp major. The first movement is in modified rondo form, the first phrase appearing more than twelve times.

6. No. 6 (E-flat) opens with a set of variations on an allegretto theme. Adagio Fantasia (2nd mvt.) in B (first part has no key signature, accidentals are written for each note), with modulations to E, G, B-flat, A-flat and back to B. Minuet uses ascending and descending E-flat major scale through all parts.

F. Op. 77 (1790): 2 quartets in G and F. Dedicated to Prince Lobkowitz

1. Transcribed by Haydn from his sonatas for flute and piano.

2. Experiments in the use of forms, thematic development, and key relationships suggest the influence of C. P. E. Bach. Some use of chromaticism in both quartets.
3. No. 1 (G): second theme (meas. 41) is omitted in the recapitulation
   of the first movement; symphonic treatment of ideas in first movement.
   Adagio (second movement) has an unusual key relationship (G and E-
   flat). Usual repeats in Minuet Trio are omitted; repetition written
   out with several changes in use of material.
4. No. 2 (F): Minuet in F, Trio in D-flat, with coda (brief but formal)
   modulating back to F by use of first Minuet theme in key of Trio.
   Andante begins with two parts only; developed into a series of highly
   ornamented variations.

G. Op. 103 (1803): Slow movement and Minuet only.
  1. Usually referred to as in the key of B-flat, but from key of Minuet
   should be called d minor, since Haydn wrote his minuets in tonic key
   of quartet. Keys in main sections of first movement (Andante grazioso): B-flat, G-flat to D-flat, c-sharp (same as d-flat), B-flat.

BIBLIOGRAPHY
General References for all Outlines

1. Altmann, W.   Kammermusik-Katalog. Leipzig: Hofmeister, 1945.
   (C.S.ML128 C4A4.8)

2. Aulich, B. and E. Heimeran. The Well-Tempered String Quartet. Transl. by D.
   M. Craig. New York: H. W. Gray, 1938. (ML67 A924sC)

3. Cobbett, W. W.   Cyclopedic Survey of Chamber Music, 2 vols. London: Oxford University Press, 1929. (ML1100 C654)

4. Dunhill, T. F.   Chamber Music. London: Macmillan & Co., 1913. (MT71 D91)

5. Grove, Sir George. Grove's Dictionary of Music and Musicians. Fifth edition edited by Eric Blom. London: Macmillan & Co., 1954.

6. Kilburn, N.   The Story of Chamber Music. New York: Charles Scribner's Sons, 1932. (ML1154 K48.2)

7. Thompson, O.   International Cyclopedia of Music and Musicians. New
   York: Dodd, Mead and Co., 1946. (ML1100 T474.3)

8. Tovey, D. F.   Essays in Musical Analysis; Vol. VII, Chamber Music.
   London: Oxford University Press, 1937. (MT90 T736)

9. Ulrich, H.   Chamber Music. New York: Columbia University Press,
   1948. (ML100 U45)

Books

1. Brenet, M. (Bobillier, Marie) Haydn. Transl. by C. L. Leese. London: Oxford University Press, 1926. (ML410 H41B66L)

2. Fox, D. G. A.   Haydn. London: Oxford University Press, 1929.
   (MT92 H41F79)

3. Geiringer, K.   Haydn, a Creative Life in Music. New York: W. W. Norton,
   1946. (ML410 H41G31H)

4. Hadden, J. C.   Haydn. New York: E. P. Dutton and Co., 1934.

(ML410 H41H12.2)

5. Hadow, W. H.   A Croatian Composer; notes toward the study of Joseph
        Haydn. London: Seeley and Co., 1897. (ML410 H41H13)

6. Jacob, H. E.   Joseph Haydn, His Art, Times, and Glory. Transl. by R.
        and C. Winston. London: Gollancz, 1950.   (ML410 H41J15)

7. Nohl, L.   Letters of Distinguished Musicians: Gluck, Haydn, C. P.
        E. Bach, Weber, Mendelssohn. Transl. by Lady Wallace. London: Longmans,
        Green & Co., 1867.

8. Nohl, L.   Life of Haydn. Transl. by G. P. Upton. Chicago: Jansen,
        McClurg and Co., 1902.   (ML410 H41N.7)

9. Pohl, C. F.   Joseph Haydn, 3 vols. Berlin: A. Sacco Nachfolger,
        1875-1927.   (ML410 H41P74)

10. Pohl, K. F.   Mozart and Haydn in London. Vienna: C. Gerolds Sohn,
        1867.

11. Tovey, D. F.   Essays and Lectures on Music. London: Oxford University
        Press, 1949. Haydn's Chamber Music. (ML60 T736e)

12. Townsend, P. D.   Joseph Haydn. London: S. Low and Co., 1894.
        (ML410 H41T74)

Periodicals

1. Adler, G.   "Haydn and the Viennese Classical School," MQ 18 (1932),
        191.

2. Botstiber, H.   "Haydn and Luigia Polzelli," MQ 18 (1932), 208.

3. Fry, J.   "Haydn's String Quartets Op. 20," MT (1944), 140.

4. Muller, J.   "Haydn Portraits," MQ 18 (1932), 282.

5. Scott, M.   "Haydn's Chamber Music," MT (1932), 212.

6. Scott, M.   "Haydn's '83': A study of the Complete Editions," ML
        (1930), 207.

7. Scott, M.   "Haydn in England," MQ 18 (1932), 260.

8. Silbert, D.   "Ambiguity in the String Quartets of Joseph Haydn,"
        MQ 36 (1950), 562.

9. Smith, C. S.   "Haydn's Chamber Music and the Flute," MQ 19 (1933),
        341, 434.

10. Strunk, W. C.   "Haydn's Divertimenti for Baryton, Viola and Bass,"
        MQ 18 (1932), 218.

11. Willfort, E. H.   "Haydn's Compositions for Mechanical Instruments," MT
        73 (1932), 510

Music

I. String Quartets
The student should own scores of the quartets selected for detailed study.

1. The Chamber Music of Haydn and Schubert, ed. Wier. New York: Longmans, Green and Co., 1940.

2. Quartets, 30 Celebrated, for 2 violins, viola and villoncello. Scarsdale, N. Y.: E. F. Kalmus Orchestra Scores, Inc., 193-? (M451 H41MD)

3. Quartets, 30 Celebrated String-. Scarsdale, N. Y.: E. F. Kalmus, 194-? (M451 H41Km)

4. Quartette, Saemmtliche, für 2 Violinen, Viola und Violoncell. Leipzig: Kistner, 189-. (M451 H41J)

5. Quatuors, Collection de, pour 2 violons, viola et violoncelle. Leipzig: Peters, 186-? (M451 H41P)

6. Quatuors, pour 2 violons, alto et violoncelle. Braunschweig & New York: H. Litolff, 187-? (M451 H41L)

7. Sämmtliche 83 Streichquartette, 3 vols. Leipzig: Eulenberg Kleine Partitur-Ausgabe, 1931. (M451 H41m.2)

II. Trios

   A. Violin, Cello and Piano

8. Grand Trio pour le clavecin ou piano forte accompagné d'un violon & violon-celle. Berlin: J. J. Hummel, 1790? (M312 H415t)

9. Five Celebrated Trios for Violin, Cello & Piano, ed. Hermann. New York: International Music Co., 1946. (M312 H415THI)

10. Trois grand trios pour le clavecin ou piano forte avec l'accompagnement de violon & violoncelle. Berlin: J. J. Hummel, 1790? (M312 H415t.6)

11. Trois Sonates pour le Piano Forte avec Accompagnement de Violon & Violoncelle. London: Preston & Son, 1792? (M312 H415t.18)

12. Trios für Pianoforte, Violine und Violoncell. Braunschweig: H. Litolff, 186-. (M312 H415TL)

13. Trios für Piano, Violine und Violoncell, ed. Hermann. Leipzig: Peters, 188-. (M312 H415TH)

   B. Violin, Viola and Cello

14. Drei Trios für Violine, Viola und Violoncello, ed. Sandberger. Braunschweig: H. Litolff, 1934. (M351 H415t.35)

15. Three Trios for Violin, Viola, & Cello. New York: International Music Co., 1948. (M351 H415t.371)

16. Trio für Violine, Viola, und Cello, ed. Geiringer. Copenhagen: W. Hansen, 1933. (M353 H415)

   C. Miscellaneous

17. Six Trios, pour flûte, violon & violoncelle. Berlin: N. Simrock, 187-. (M361 H41)

18. __Trio in A major__, arr. Tovey. London: Oxford University Press, 1939.
       (M312 H415t.7T)

| | Records | | |
| Title | Music | Recording | Call No. |

I. String Quartets
    The abbreviation "W" refers to __The Chamber Music of Haydn and Schubert__, ed.
    Wier (M 1)

1. Op. 1, Nos. 0, 1, 2, 3, 4, 6		HSQ-A (Schneider)	
a. No. 1	W, 8		
b. No. 6	W, 11		
2. Op. 2, Nos. 1-6		HSQ-B (Schneider)	
3. Op. 3, No. 5	W, 15	Lond LS-656 (Griller)	
		Angel D35185 (New Italian)	
		West 5064/65 (Amadeus)	
4. Op. 17, Nos. 1-6		HSQ-E (Schneider)	
5. Op. 20, Nos. 1-6		HSQ-F (Schneider)	
a. No. 1	W, 19		
b. No. 2	W, 23		
c. No. 4	W, 28		
d. No. 5	W, 35		
6. Op. 33, Nos. 1-6		HSQ-G (Schneider)	
a. No. 2	W, 42		
b. No. 3	W, 46		
c. No. 6	W, 52		
7. Op. 42		HSQ-M (Schneider)	
8. Op. 50, Nos. 1-6		HSQ-H (Schneider)	
a. No. 3	W, 56		
9. Op. 51 (Seven Last Words)		HSQ 39 (Schneider)	
10. Op. 54, No. 2		All 58 (Kroll)	
11. Op. 54, No. 3	W, 67	Vic M-528 (Pro Arte)	
12. Op. 55, No. 1	W, 74	Vic M-528 (Pro Arte)	
13. Op. 55, No. 3	W, 78	Vic M-595	
14. Op. 64, Nos. 1-6			
a. No. 1		West 5314 (Vienna)	
b. No. 3		West 5314 (Vienna)	
c. No. 4	W, 82	Vic M-528	
d. No. 5	W, 88	Blue LBC-1073 (American)	
		Col 3ML-4216 (Budapest)	

15. Op. 71, No. 1	W, 99	Vic M-525
16. Op. 74, No. 2	W, 105	Per 503 (Baroque)
17. Op. 74, No. 3	W, 113	Ura 7-20 (di Roma)
18. Op. 76, Nos. 1-6		HSQ-L (Schneider) Col 4SL-203 (Budapest)
a. No. 3	W, 119	HSQ 35
b. No. 4	W, 126	HSQ 36
c. No. 5	W, 131	HSQ 36
19. Op. 77		
a. No. 1	W, 137	HSQ 37 (Schneider) EMS 301 (B. Heifitz) All 58 (Kroll
b. No. 2	W, 145	HSQ 38 (Schneider) EMS 301 (B. Heifitz)
20. Op. 103		HSQ 38 (Schneider) West 5064/65 (Amadeus)

II. Trios

21. Trios for Two Flutes, Cello (London) a. Nos. 1-4		All 48
22. Trios for Violin, Cello, Piano		
a. Nos. 1 (G), 28 (G), 30 (D)		West 5202
b. Nos. 4 (E), 17 (E-flat), 27 (F), 29 (F)		West 5293
c. Nos. 3 (C), 2 (f-sharp), 5 (E-flat)		Dec DX-104
23. Trios for Strings a. Op. 53, Nos. 1 (G), 2 (B-flat), 3 (D)		West 5296
24. Three Trios for Piano, Flute, Cello		Ois 50036
25. Trio for Horn in E-flat		HS 1044

OUTLINE III
WOLFGANG AMADEUS MOZART (1756 - 1791)

I. Life

    1756 Born at Salzburg, Austria, January 27.

    1760 Clavier lessons begun with father; first pieces composed (1761).

    1762 Visited Munich, Vienna, Pressburg with his father and sister.

    1763 Salzburg; Mozarts (Wolfgang, father, sister) began a concert tour in
          June, going to Belgium, Holland, France, Switzerland. Entertained at
          Versailles by Louis XV; played at the court in London; met J. C. Bach.
          Returned to Salzburg (1766).

    1769 Italy; studied with Padre Martini; began to compose quartets.

    1771 Salzburg; Italy.

    1772 Salzburg; active period of composition; Milan.

    1773 Salzburg; Vienna, Milan, Munich. Quartets K. 168-173 written in
          Viennese style. He composed no more quartets until 1782.

    1776 Salzburg; difficulties with the Archbishop.

    1777 Mannheim; met Weber family.

    1778 Paris; met J. C. Bach again. Returned to Salzburg by way of Mannheim
          and Munich.

    1781 Famous contest with Clementi at Court of Prince-Archbishop of Salz-
          burg. First meeting with Haydn in Vienna.

    1782 Began composition of the "Haydn" quartets. Married Constanze Weber,
          August 4 and made Vienna their home. From this time until his death,
          Mozart was without a regular position and his life was one of dis-
          appointment, discouragement and poverty.

    1784 Vienna; met Sarti and Paisiello; Salzburg, Linz.

    1787 Prague; Vienna (met Beethoven).

    1789 Visited Dresden, Leipzig, Berlin, with Prince Lichnowsky.

    1790 Played the "Coronation" Piano Concerto (D Major) at Frankfurt.

    1791 Vienna; received a mysterious commission for a <u>Requiem</u>. Died December
          5, the <u>Requiem</u> unfinished, and was buried in a pauper's grave.

II. Catalogue of Chamber Music

    A. String instruments
        1. Quartets
            a. 26 for 2 violins, viola, cello.
        2. Quintets
            a. 5 for 2 violins, 2 violas, cello.
        3. Trios
            a. 1 for violin, viola, cello.
            b. 1 for 2 violins, bass, continuo.
        4. Duos
            a. 2 for violin, viola.
    B. Piano and other instruments
        1. 42 sonatas for violin, piano.
        2. Trios
            a. 7 for piano, violin, cello.
            b. 1 for piano, clarinet, viola.

    3. Quartets
       a. 2 for piano, violin, viola, cello.
    4. Quintet
       a. Piano, oboe, clarinet, horn, bassoon.
  C. String and wind instruments
    1. 5 Divertimenti.
    2. 3 quartets
       a. 2 for flute, violin, viola, cello.
       b. 1 for oboe, violin, viola, cello.
    3. 2 quintets
       a. 1 for 2 violins, viola, cello, clarinet.
       b. 1 for violin, 2 violas, cello, horn.
    4. 1 duet for bassoon, cello.
  D. Wind instruments
    1. 12 duets for 2 horns.
    2. 5 Divertimenti for 2 clarinets, bassoon.
    3. Miscellaneous works with basset-horn.

III. Chamber Music

  A. Within the short space of thirty-six years, Mozart proved himself the most comprehensive genius who ever lived, bringing to everything he touched the perfection of a master. The best-known qualities of his music are brightness, gayety and serenity. There is, however, a deeper, more tragic note, an underlying tenderness and melancholy.
    1. One of the least nationalistic of the great composers, Mozart, in spirit and style, was more Italian than German. Working instinctively, he brought unlimited resourcefulness to each form of creative music.
  B. Mozart received his early training from his father, an excellent musician and teacher, and the author of a famous violin method.
    1. In his visits to Paris and London, he became acquainted with the music of Johann Schobert and Johann Christian Bach.
    2. He knew the <u>Gradus ad Parnassum</u> of Fux as early as 1766 and became thoroughly familiar with the contrapuntal style of German and Austrian composers.
    3. He was strongly influenced by the light, melodious, and spontaneous Rococo style found in the works of Sammartini, Johann Christian Bach and others.
  C. Mozart composed chamber music throughout his life. His first violin sonata was written at the age of seven, his last quintet in the year of his death.
    1. The style and form of chamber music was not clearly defined when he began to compose. By the time of his death, however, chamber and symphonic styles had become completely separated and sonata-form and over-all forms were established, though both were still capable of expansion.
    2. Chamber works form roughly about one-fifth of Mozart's total compositions. His progress as a composer may be most clearly seen in the violin sonatas, written from his earliest to most mature period.
  D. The 26 quartets may be divided into two large groups, which may in turn be subdivided.
    1. K.80, K. 136-138, K. 155-160, K. 168-173 (1770-73).
    2. The six "Haydn," the "Hoffmeister," and the three "Prussian" quartets (1782-90).

IV. Early String Quartets (1770-73)

  A. Show the influence of other composers on his style; foreshadow devices that are associated with his mature works and show the growth of the formal aspects of his style.
    1. K. 50 (G) (1770)
       a. Not a true quartet. Originally only three movements; the Rondo

was added in 1773. Written during his first visit to Italy. The influence of Sammartini and the North-Italian trio-sonata is seen in the large number of short melodies and the arrangement of tempos in the movements (Adagio, Allegro, Minuet with Trio), the unity of key, and the general homophonic style.
   b. The first violin has most of the melodic material; second violin has many passages in sixths, thirds and tenths with the first; viola and cello have accompaniment figures.
2. Three Quartets (1772): K. 136 (D), K. 137 (B-flat), K. 138 (F)
   a. Written in Salzburg. They were designated "divertimenti" on the original manuscript (probably not by Mozart), but are unlike divertimenti in having only three movements and no minuets. Possibly intended to be used either as quartets, or, with the addition of horn and oboe parts, as symphonies.
   b. Principal interest lies in the two violin parts; two lower parts consist mostly of repeated quarter notes marking the harmony. Opening themes are often built on tonic chord figures. Fast movements have sudden changes of dynamics; final cadences often end with repeated chords.
   c. Developments are sectional; one theme is used before going to the next. Material not always literal; may be only a rhythmic recalling of material used in the exposition or new material.
   d. Sonata-forms mostly three-part, but with short developments. K. 138 introduces a new subject in the development. Andante (K. 138) is in two-part form; first theme appears immediately after the double bar in the key of the dominant, followed by the second theme in the tonic key.
   e. K. 137 has the same key throughout the three movements; K. 136 and K. 138 have a middle movement in contrasting key.
   f. K. 137 shows Mozart's skill in handling the return of the second theme in the recapitulation of the first movement.
3. Six Quartets (1772-73): K. 155 (D), K. 156 (G), K. 157 (C), K. 158 (F), K. 159 (B-flat), K. 160 (E-flat).
   a. Keys in a circle of fourths. All have three movements. First movement fast, second slow, except K. 159 which reverses the order.
   b. Concertante style, first and second violins against viola and cello, or solo violin against second violin and viola with cello as continuo. First and second violins have many passages in thirds, sixths, octaves, and tenths.
   c. Dynamics apt to be strongly and suddenly contrasted (Mannheim influence). Developments sectional.
   d. More interest in lower voices; first theme announced by second violin (K. 159); cello uses imitation (K. 159).
   e. Greater contrast between first and second themes than before.
4. Six Quartets (1773): K. 168 (F), K. 169 (A), K. 170 (C), K. 171 (E-flat), K. 172 (B-flat), K. 173 (d).
   a. In Viennese style. Written after Mozart knew Haydn's Op. 17 and Op. 20, and are strongly influenced by these. New features include: four-movement form; contrapuntal texture and resultant independence and importance of the three lower instruments; thematic instead of sectional developments; a new economy of material (a transitional passage, for instance, may grow out of a figure in the first theme).
   b. Other indications of Haydn's influences are: use of slow introduction (K. 171); fugue for the last movement (K. 168, K. 173); typical Haydn nine-measure period divided into 3-2-2-2 phrases (K. 168); first movement (K. 170) an Andante with variations.
   c. Foreshadowings of Mozart's later style are seen in the chromaticism in the last part of some of the main themes (K. 168, the Minuet of K. 170), and in the use of a third relationship between the main theme and transition of the Andante of K. 169.

V. Late Quartets (1782-90)

  A. Mozart wrote no string quartets between 1773 and 1782. In the meantime, Haydn brought out six quartets, Op. 33 (1781). Mozart studied them and was profoundly impressed. In these nine years his harmonic style had matured; he had written, among other things, twelve symphonies and one important opera (Idomeneo).

  B. His later quartets have all of the characteristics of his mature style: use of short chromatic lines, harmonic freedom, perfection of form, closely knit contrapuntal texture. Some characteristics of earlier works are still present: doublings in tenths, thirds, sixths; preference for the subdominant key for the slow movement. Codas are often longer and more developed.

  C. Six "Haydn" Quartets (1782-85): K. 387 (G), K. 421 (d), K. 428 (E-flat), K. 458 (B-flat), K. 464 (A), K. 465 (C).

    1. These six quartets and the last four are also known as the "Ten Celebrated Quartets."

    2. Mozart's dedication begins: "To my dear friend Haydn! A father who has concluded to send his children into the world at large, thought best to entrust them to the protection and guidance of a famous man who fortunately happened to be his best friend as well."

    3. K. 387 (G)

      a. Allegro vivace assai (G). Sonata-form.

        1) Exposition (meas. 1-55); principal section (meas. 1-24); 1st subject alternates diatonic and chromatic motives (meas. 1-4); viola introduces a motive (meas. 5) which is answered by 2nd and 1st violin; subsidiary section (meas. 25-38); 2nd theme (meas. 25-26) in dominant; viola doubles violin at 10th (meas. 31-34); closing section (meas. 39-55).

        2) Development (meas. 56-107); motive of 1st theme in violin (D) (meas. 56), 2nd violin (e) (meas. 61), viola (C) (meas. 68); imitation of scale-like motive in violins (meas. 70-79); dotted note figure at end of Exposition (meas. 54-55) repeated in e (meas. 88-89) and in same key (D) (meas. 99-100); imitative trill passage leads to a V_7 chord and the Recapitulation.

        3) Recapitulation (meas. 108-170); varied treatment of material of Exposition; 2nd theme in tonic as usual.

      b. Menuetto-Allegro (G-g). Modified sonata-form.

        1) First subject diatonic (meas. 1-2) followed by chromatic scale lines with alternating p-f which produces a 2-beat effect; 2nd subject in dominant (meas. 21). 2nd section begins with a short development and a recapitulation follows (meas. 63) with a return of the 2nd subject in the tonic (meas. 74). Trio in g uses an ascending arpeggio trill motive; some imitative writing in the 2nd section.

      c. Andante cantabile (C). Modified sonata-form.

        1) Exposition (meas. 1-51) divided into a principal section (meas. 1-30), subsidiary section (meas. 30-46); closing section (meas. 46-48) leads to a short transitory passage (meas. 48-51) which replaces the Development.

        2) Recapitulation (meas. 51-106) varies the Exposition with special emphasis on the repeated-note motive; 2nd theme (meas. 87-88) in tonic.

      d. Molto allegro (G). Free sonata-form with fugued sections.

        1) Exposition (meas. 1-125); principal section (meas. 1-51) begins with a fugal exposition (meas. 1-17); subject recalls fugue of "Jupiter" Symphony; free responsive section (meas. 17-51); responsive section concludes with a chromatic passage with a pedal point on A varied at end (meas. 39-51). Subsidiary section (meas. 51-107); fugal exposition of the 2nd subject (meas. 51-68) which is combined with 1st fugue subject (meas. 69-91); solo section corresponding to 1st free section (meas. 92-106);

closing section (meas. 107-119); transitory passage leading, with a chromatic motive (meas. 120-124), to the Development.

2) Development (meas. 125-174) opens with the chromatic motive; 1st fugue subject reappears in 1st violin and cello, passing through remote keys (meas. 143-159).

3) Recapitulation (meas. 175-266) has no clearly defined starting point (Beethoven); begins with free responsive section in sub-dominant; 2nd subject in tonic combined with 1st fugue subject (meas. 209-234); solo section in tonic (meas. 235-242); closing section and transitory passage lead to coda.

4) Coda (meas. 266-298) begins with chromatic motive of Development; stretto of 1st fugue subject in 1st violin, viola, cello (meas. 282-287).

4. K. 421 (d)

  a. Allegro (d). Sonata-form.

    1) Exposition (meas. 1-41); principal section and modulation (meas. 1-24); subsidiary section (meas. 25-35); 2nd theme in relative major (F) (meas. 25-26); closing section (meas. 35-41); codetta fugue in 1st violin (meas. 39) used in Development.

    2) Development (meas. 42-69) begins suddenly in E-flat with 2-meas. motive of 1st theme; dissonant imitation (meas. 53-58); use of codetta figure at end of Exposition (meas. 59-70).

    3) Recapitulation (meas. 70-112) has slight alteration of material; 2nd theme in d, slightly varied (meas. 94-95).

    4) Coda (meas. 112-117) short; use of codetta motive.

  b. Andante (F). Ternary form with Coda.

    1) Pt. I (meas. 1-26), principal section (meas. 1-8), middle section (meas. 9-14), expanded recapitulation of principal section (meas. 15-26). Pt. II (meas. 26-51) a free variation of theme. Pt. III a recapitulation of Pt. I (meas. 52-77). Coda (meas. 77-86).

  c. Menuetto (d-D)

    1) Serious style. Contrasting Trio uses unusual 16th-and dotted-8th note rhythm; rare use of pizzicato (only important use in any of Mozart's string quartets).

  d. Allegro ma non troppo (d)

    1) Theme and 4 variations in "Siciliano" rhythm. Variation 4 in D. Coda (meas. 113-142) returns to theme with some alterations.

5. K. 428 (E-flat)

  a. Allegro begins with the theme in unison; 2nd theme (meas. 40) finally establishes dominant (B-flat). Development section uses 1st theme in canon and 1st motive of 2nd theme. Andante (A-flat) is in sonata-form with a short development section. Minuet Trio (B-flat) uses pedal points on C, B-flat, G, F, B-flat. Finale (Allegro vivace) (E-flat) is in style of Haydn; Rondo form based largely on material from meas. 1-8 and 60-67.

6. K. 458 (B-flat)

  a. Horn call at opening gave name of the "Hunt" quartet; 2nd theme (meas. 54). Development begins with a new theme (meas. 91) in F, ending in f (meas. 106). Recapitulation (meas. 138-231) is followed by an unusually long Coda (meas. 232-279) which uses the hunting theme in imitative passages. Minuet the 2nd mvt.

  b. Adagio (E-flat) movement used for the only time in the "Haydn" quartets. Sonata-form; principal section (mea. 1-14); contrasting 2nd theme (meas. 15).

  c. Finale is in sonata-form (possibly rondo) with 3 subjects: 1) meas. 1-4; 2) meas. 48-50; 3) meas. 82-85. Closing section of Exposition (meas. 81-121) and coda (meas. 122-133). Development (meas. 134-199) is based on 1st subject. Recapitulation (meas. 200-319) uses all 3 subjects in tonic key (B-flat). Coda (meas. 320-335).

7. K. 464 (A)

7. K. 464 (A)
 a. Principal theme is in a new style; based on two motives; use of
chromaticism; unison passage based on principal theme (meas. 9-12);
key of dominant reached through C and an augmented sixth on C (meas.
32). 2nd subject begins in meas. 37. <u>Development</u> (meas. 88-161)
based largely on principal theme and unison theme of meas. 9-12.
<u>Recapitulation</u> (meas. 162-270).
 b. Minuet (A-E) based on 2 melodic sequences which are combined (meas.
9-12), and used in canonic imitation and inversion. Trio in E.
 c. Andante (D) is a theme (divided into 2 parts, each repeated) with
6 variations and a Coda variation. Variation VI is built over a
strongly rhythmic dominant pedal which is also used in the Coda.
 d. Finale (A) opens with a chromatic motive and makes frequent use of
sequences. Sonata-form with 2nd subject almost identical with 1st
subject (meas. 40-45) which gives the effect of only one main theme.
<u>Exposition</u> (meas. 82-144) based mostly on 2nd subject; interrupted
by a chorale-like section (meas. 114) which uses chromatic 1st
motive in augmentation (meas. 118-119). <u>Recapitulation</u> begins in
meas. 145; 2nd subject returns in tonic (meas. 185). <u>Coda</u> (meas.
230-262).

8. K. 465 (C)
 a. Contains the famous "dissonant" chromatic introduction; parts written in "linear" style. Slow introduction to the 1st mvt. is unique;
only one in the series; unity in style and temperament is achieved
by melodic chromaticism and the device of melodic reiteration of
tones -- both being characteristics of all movements.
 b. Unusual features are: a beginning vague in harmonic intent; cross
relations (meas. 2, 6); change of mode in Minuet (C to c).
 c. In the final mvt. are found third relationships (meas. 88-89; 291-
292), canonic writing between 1st violin and cello (D-flat) with
imitation at a distance of 3 octaves (meas. 308-318).

D. K. 499 in D (1786). Dedicated to Franz Anton Hoffmeister.
 1. During 1786 Mozart was writing <u>The Marriage of Figaro</u> and composed
only one string quartet. The quartet shows freedom within the sonata-
form (development passages at unexpected places in both 1st and last
mvts.); freedom in modulation (development of 1st mvt. has a series of
modulations from a to E-flat and then to D by means of the enharmonic
nature of V_7 of E-flat and German-sixth of D).

E. Three Prussian Quartets (1789-90): K. 575 (D), K. 589 (B-flat), K. 590
(F).
 1. Commissioned by King Frederick William II of Prussia, an amateur
cellist. As a result the cello is prominent, sometimes solo (Minuet
K. 575); frequently in high range, even reaching e".

V. Five String Quintets

A. Mozart first became acquainted with the quintet in Italy, from the works
of Sammartini. Later, in Salzburg, he knew the similar works of Michael
Haydn. Mozart's first quintet, scored for 2 violins, 2 violas, cello,
was written in 1773. He did not again use the form until fourteen years
later when his style had reached maturity.

B. K. 174 (B-flat) (1773)
 1. First two movements are written in Italian style; last two were re-
vised after Mozart became acquainted with the works of Michael Haydn;
work stylistically uneven.

C. K. 515 (C), K. 516 (g) (1787)
 1. These two quintets form a pair; strongly contrasted in key (C and g)
and mood. Writing is generally for two concertante groups. These
may be violins and first viola against violas and cello (first viola
belonging to both groups), or violin and cello against the other
instruments.

  2. C-major quintet light in tone quality. The first movement is in son-
     ata-form with all sections extended and with certain "romantic"
     tendencies (main theme repeated immediately in key of the parallel
     minor, followed by a modulation to A-flat). Last movement has develop-
     ment section between the themes in the recapitulation and several in-
     stances of enharmonic modulation.
  3. G-minor quintet more sombre, even though it ends in G major. Chroma-
     tic first movement theme, and like C major, has both first and last
     movements extended.
D. K. 593 (D) (1790), K. 614 (E-flat) (1791)
  1. Last two quintets show a stricter concentration of thematic material
     and a more contrapuntal texture. Also more "romantic" in harmony and
     modulations.
  2. K. 593 in D has a slow introduction before an Allegro whose second
     subject is a canonic variation of the first. Last movement is full of
     contrapuntal devices. In the Recapitulation the main subject serves
     as a counterpoint to the second subject.
  3. K. 614 in E-flat also has a contrapuntal last movement. Rondo-type,
     with development passages instead of new themes; full of fugatos, in-
     versions, etc. First movement somewhat contrapuntal with busy trills
     and sixteenth notes. Second theme (meas. 39) answered by cello (meas.
     46). Relatively short development. Andante a combination of con-
     certante and chamber-music elements. "A combination of brilliance,
     workmanship, repose and joy in creation." Minuet has a bagpipe trio;
     in style of Haydn, as is Finale.

VI. Trios and Duos
   A. K. 266 (B-flat) (1776), for 2 violins, cello.
     1. A duet for two violins with continuo; two movements: Adagio, Minuet.
   B. Divertimento in E-flat, for violin, viola, cello, K. 563 (1788)
     1. Typical divertimento, 2ith six movements, two of which are minuets.
        Writing mostly in strict three-part style, without double-stops.
   C. Two Duos for violin and viola, K. 423 (G), K. 424 (B-flat) (1783)
     1. Three movements each; viola often uses double-stops; both instruments
        share in thematic material. Said to have been written for Michael
        Haydn.

VII. Piano with Other Instruments

   A. Trios with Piano.
     1. Trios for piano, violin and cello.
        a. K. 254 (B-flat) (1776)
          1) Little more than a piano sonata with string accompaniment.
             Violin rarely has melodic material, usually lies below right
             hand of piano part. Cello generally doubles the piano bass.
        b. K. 442 (d) (1783)
          1) More advanced in the style of the string parts; finished by
             Mozart's friend Stadler. Three movements, last in the key of
             the parallel major.
        c. K. 496 (G), K. 502 (B-flat) (1786)
          1) Written in the same year as the "Hoffmeister" quartet and in the
             same period as the three great violin sonatas.
          2) Cello more important; tendency toward virtuosity in piano parts.
             Both have three movements.
        d. K. 542 (E), K. 548 (C), K. 564 (G) (1788)
          1) Usually begin with piano alone; develop themes of secondary im-
             portance; have virtuoso piano parts; three movements. K. 564
             originally intended as a piano sonata.
     2. K. 498 (E-flat) (1786)
        a. Trio for piano, clarinet, viola. Work is based on contrast between

the viola and clarinet. Three movements.
- B. Quartets with Piano.
  - 1. K. 478 (g) (1785), K. 493 (E-flat) (1786)
    - a. First quartets with piano in real chamber-music style. Both have three movements: Allegro in sonata-form; a slow movement in sonata-form; a typical Mozart Rondo (A-B-A-C-B-A).
- C. Quintet for Piano and Winds, K. 452 (E-flat) (1784).
  - 1. Mozart wrote six piano concertos in 1784, and the quintet reflects the concerto in its virtuoso piano part.
  - 2. Winds include oboe, clarinet, horn, bassoon. Concertante style, with the piano against the wind instruments. Wind group itself is divided into various concertante groups.
  - 3. Three movements: opening Allegro preceded by a Largo introduction. Rondo finale has concerto-like cadenza played by all instruments. Mozart wrote his father that it was "the best work I have ever composed."

VIII. String and Wind Instruments.
- A. Five Divertimenti.
  - 1. Basic instrumentation is a string quartet and two horns. Two divertimenti add another instrument to this. Divertimenti are much lighter than other chamber music; often written to celebrate some special occasion. All except one (K. 251) have six movements, including two minuets. Slow movements usually omit horns. First violin definitely a virtuoso instrument. Four divertimenti are to be preceded and followed by a March, which the players performed as they entered and left the room. K. 287 was written for winter performance, so has no March.
  - 2. "Vienna" Divertimenti (1773): K. 205 (D).
    - a. Bassoon added, doubling cello part. Key of D is used for all except the slow movement. March (K. 290) precedes and follows the six movements.
  - 3. "Salzburg" Divertimenti (1776-77): K. 247 (F), K. 287 (B-flat), K. 334 (D).
    - a. K. 247 adds the March, K. 248. K. 334 is also to be played with a March, possibly K. 445. In K. 251, which adds an oboe to the instrumentation, the March is inscribed "Marcia illa française." K. 287 has for its last movement a Rondo built on the South German popular song "Die Bauerin hat die Katz verlorn." This is preceded and followed by comic recitative, a parody on operatic style.
- B. Four Quartets for Flute, Violin, Viola, Cello (1777, 1778): K. 285 (D), K. 285a (G), K. 285b (C) (Anh. 171), K. 298 (A).
  - 1. Mozart was commissioned by a rich amateur flute player to write three quartets with flute. Only the first of the three was completed (K. 285, in D). The flute part is prominent, but only in the second movement is it a solo instrument. This movement, Adagio, has an accompaniment of pizzicato strings. Unfinished quartets K. 285a and K. 285b (Anh. 171), have only two movements.
  - 2. K. 298, in three movements, is a parody on the "foreign" music of his time.
- C. Quartet for Oboe, Violin, Viola, Cello (1781): K. 370 (F).
  - 1. Composed for the oboist Friedrich Ramm of Mannheim in the year of Idomeneo. One of Mozart's best works. Three movements; slow movement has a short cadenza for oboe; in final Rondo the oboe is sometimes in 4/4 and the other instruments in 6/8 (meas. 95).
- D. Two Quintets.
  - 1. Quintet for Horn, Violin, 2 Violas, Cello (1783): K. 407 (E-flat).
    - a. Three movements, each in a different style. In the first movement the horn and violin are more in the nature of solo instruments; the other strings act as an accompaniment. The second

movement is semi-contrapuntal; short canonic passages throughout. Final Rondo has a virtuoso part for horn; suggests concerto style, with horn solos and tutti passages.

    2. Quintet for Clarinet and String Quartet (1789): K. 581 (A).
      a. More in chamber style than horn quintet. Four movements; Minuet has two trios, first movement omits clarinet; last movement is an air and variations instead of a Rondo.

E. Sonata for Bassoon and Cello (1775): K. 292 (B-flat).
    1. Three movements. Instruments are not treated equally; cello given secondary place.

IX. Wind Instruments

A. 12 Duets for Two Horns (1786): K. 487
    1. Formerly thought to be for two basset-horns. Slight, though tuneful, little pieces with the following titles: (1) Allegro, (2) Minuet, (3) Andante, (4) Polonaise, (5) Larghetto, (6) Minuet, (7) Adagio, (8) Allegro, (9) Minuet, (10) Andante, (11) Minuet, (12) Allegro.

B. 5 Divertimenti for Two Clarinets and Bassoon (1783-85): K. Anh. 229.
    1. Slight works; in key of B-flat; all have five movements. First three have the same general form: Allegro-Minuet-Slow movement-Minuet-Rondo. Last two have only one Minuet; No. 4 has two slow movements; No. 5 has a Polonaise and a Romanze for the last two movements. Little key change between the movements; only one movement in each divertimento is in a different key; this key is always the key of the dominant or subdominant.

C. Miscellaneous works with Basset Horn.
    1. Canonic Adagio for Two Basset Horns and Bassoon (1782): K. 410 (F).
      a. A very short work. Bassoon is merely an accompanying part; canon between the basset horns.
    2. Adagio for Two Clarinets and Three Basset Horns (1782): K. 411 (F).
      a. Concertante style; upper four instruments in various combinations against third basset horn. Sonata-form.

BIBLIOGRAPHY

Books

1. Anderson, E.   The Letters of Mozart and His Family, 3 vols. New York: Macmillan, 1938. (ML410 M93A546)

2. Berlioz, H.   Mozart, Weber, and Wagner. Transl. by E. Evans. London: W. Reeves, 1918. (ML410 B41ME)

3. Biancolli, L.P., ed. The Mozart Handbook; a guide to the man and his music. Cleveland: World Publishing Co., 1954. (ML410 M93B57)

4. Blom, E.   Mozart. New York: E. P. Dutton and Co., 1944. (ML410 M93B65)

5. Breakspeare, E. J. Mozart. London: J. M. Dent & Co.; New York: E. P. Dutton & Co., 1902. (ML410 M93B82)

6. Cowen, Sir F. H. Mozart. London: Murdoch, Murdoch & Co., 190-. (ML410 M93C87)

7. Dunhill, T.F.   Mozart's String Quartets. Books I and II. New York: Oxford University Press, 1927. (MT145 M93D91)

8. Einstein, A.   Mozart: His Character, His Work. Transl. by A. Mendel and

N. Broder. New York: Oxford University Press, 1945. (ML410 M93E35)

9. Ghéon, H.   In Search of Mozart. Transl. by A. Dru. New York: Sheed & Ward, Inc., 1934. (ML410 M93G41)

10. Ginzkey, F. K.   Genius Mozart. Zürich: Scientia-Verlag, 1949. (ML410 M93G49)

11. Hussey, D.   Mozart. ("Masters of Music" Series). London: Kegan Paul, Trench, Trubner & Co., 1928. (ML410M93H97)

12. Jahn, O.   Wolfgang Amadeus Mozart. Transl. by P. D. Townsend, 3 vols. London: Novello & Co., 1891. (ML410 M93J25T)

13. Kerst, F.   Mozart. The Man and the Artist as Revealed in his own Words. Transl. by H. E. Krehbiel. New York: B. W. Huebach, 1905. (ML410 M93K41)

14. Köchel, L.   Chronologisch-thematisches Verzeichnis sämtlicher Tonwerke Wolfgang Amadeus Mozarts. Rev. 3rd ed. by Alfred Einstein. Leipzig: Breitkopf & Härtel, 1937. Reprinted by J.W. Edwards, Ann Arbor, Mich., 1947. (ML134 M939K77.3E)

15. Kolb, A.   Mozart. London: V. Gollancz, Ltd., 1939. (ML410 M93K81B)

16. Mersmanns, H.   Letters of Mozart. New York: Dutton & Co., 1928. (ML410 M93M57)

17. Newman, E. W.   A Musical Critic's Holiday. New York: A. A. Knopf, 1925. pp. 131-150. (ML3915 N55)

18. Sitwell, S.   Mozart. London: P. Davies, Ltd., 1932. (ML410 M93S62)

19. Talbot, J. E.   Mozart. London: Duckworth, 1934. (ML410 M93T13)

20. Tenschert, E.   Wolfgang Amadeus Mozart. Transl. by E. Anderson. New York: Macmillan Co., 1953. (ML410 M93T31Mo)

21. Turner, W. J.   Mozart, the Man and his Works. London: V. Gollancz, Ltd., 1938. (ML410 M93T9)

22. Wilder, V.   Mozart, the Man and the Artist. Transl. by L. Liebich, 2 vols. New York: Scribner & Son, 1908. (ML410 M93W671)

Periodicals

1. Dawson, R. V.   "Haydn and Mozart," MQ 16 (1930), 498.

2. Einstein, A.   "Mozart's Choice of Keys," MQ 27 (1941), 418.

3. Einstein, A.   "Mozart's Four String Trio Preludes to Fugues of Bach," MT 77 (1936), 209.

4. Einstein, A.   "Mozart's Ten Celebrated String Quartets," MR 3 (1942),159.

5. Einstein, A.   "Mozartiana and Köcheliana," MR 1 (1940), 313, and MR 2 (1941), 68.

6. Girdlestone, C.M. "Mozart's Last Salzburg Compositions," Chesterian 16 (1934), 29.

7. Hutchings, A.J.B. "The Unexpected in Mozart," ML 20 (1939), 21.

8. King, A.H.   "The Fragmentary Works of Mozart," MT 81 (1940), 401.

9. King, A.H.   "Mozart's Counterpoint: its Growth and Significance,"
   ML 26 (1945), 12.

10. King, A.H.   "Mozart's Prussian Quartets in Relation to his Later
    Style," ML 21 (1940), 328.

11. King, A.H.   "A Survey of Recent Mozart Literature," MR 3 (1942), 248.

12. McNaught, W. "Mozart's String Quartets. A New Edition," MT 86 (1945),
    235.

13. Mozart, W.A. "Mozart's Letters," British Musician 5 (1929), 10.

14. Oldman, C.B. "Representative Books about Mozart," ML 6 (1925), 128.

15. Phillips, H.D. "The Anomalous Place of Mozart in Music," MQ 8 (1922),372.

16. Porte, J.F.   "The Playing of Mozart," ML 7 (1926), 374.

17. Prod-homme, J.G. "The Wife of Mozart: Constanze Weber," MQ 13 (1927), 384.

18. Smith, A.B. (Brent-Smith). "A Study of Mozart," NMR 30 (1931), 165.

19. Squires, P.C. "Mozart: the Janus of Music," JAMS 3 (1941), 53.

20. Tangeman, R.S. "Mozart's Seventeen Epistle Sonatas," MQ 32 (1946), 588.

21. Ward, M.   "Mozart and the Clarinet," ML 22 (1941), 126.

22. Watson, J.A. "Mozart and the Viola," ML 22 (1941), 41.

Music

1. Wier, A.E.   The Chamber Music of Mozart. New York: Longmans, Green &
   Co., 1940.

2. Breitkopf & Härtel.
                 1) Partiturbibliothek (scores). Leipzig, 1879.
                 2) Orchesterbibliothek or Kammermusikbibliothek (parts).

		1)	2)	
a.	K. 131	1) No. 69	2) No. 2412	(M995 M939.D2, score)
b.	K. 247	1) No. 71	2) No. 2426	
c.	K. 287 (271b)			
		1) No. 73	2) No. 1823-25	(M662 M939.9)
d.	K. 166	1) No. 394	2) No. 2414	(M995 M939D.3)
e.	K. 213	1) No. 398	2) No. 2422-23	(M657 M939D.1)
f.	K. 375	1) No. 405	2) No. 1845-47	(M857 M939.7)
g.	K. 388 (384a)			
		1) No. 406	2) No. 1826-28	(M857 M939.8)
h.	K. 270	1) No. 402	2) No. 2433-34	(M657 M939D.5)

3. Eulenburg, E. Eulenbergs kleine Partitur-Ausgabe, Kammermusik (miniature
   scores only). Leipzig: E. Eulenberg, 1889.

a.	K. 247	No. 195	(M622 M939.8m)
b.	K. 251	No. 349	(M762 M939.11m)
c.	K. 375	No. 159	(M857 M939.7m)
d.	K. 388 (384a)	No. 309	(M857 M939.8m)

4. Mozart, W.A.   <u>Wolfgang Amadeus Mozarts sämtliche Werke</u>.   24 series in 75
     vols. Leipzig: Breitkopf & Härtel, 1877-1905.

5. Mozart, W.A.   <u>Individual Works</u>

   a. <u>String Quartets</u>. New York: Kalmus, 1948. (scores)
   b. <u>Die Mailänder Quartette</u>. Mainz: B. Schotts Söhne, 1932. (separate parts)
      (M451 M939W)
   c. <u>Adagio und Fuge, C moll</u>. K. 546. Leipzig: Breitkopf & Härtel, 190-.
      (<u>Quartette für Streichinstrumente</u>, Serie XIV No. 27). (M452 M93a)
   d. <u>Two Duets for Violin & Viola</u>. New York: Weaver-Levant, 1942. (separate
      parts). (M287 M939.DW)
   e. <u>Nineteen Sonatas for Violin & Piano</u>. New York: International Music Co.,
      1947. (Piano and violin parts). (M219 M93F)
   f. <u>Divertimento, No. 17 in D Major</u>, K. 334 (320b). Arr. for violin & piano
      by Jascha Heifetz. New York: Carl Fischer, 1944. (M223 M939DiH K320b)
   g. 1) <u>Duet for Bassoon & Cello</u>, K. 292 (196c). Transc. for 2 cellos by J.
         Werner. New York: International Music Co., 1947. (separate parts).
         (M287 M939SW)
      2) <u>ibid</u>. Transc. for 2 cellos by Paul Bazelaire. Paris: A. Leduc, 1923.
         (score). (M287 M939vB)
   h. <u>Adagio & Rondo in C minor</u>, K. 617. For glass harmonica (or piano), flute,
      oboe, viola and cello. New York: International Music Co., 1948. (score
      & parts). (M524 M939A)
   i. <u>Divertimenti Nos. 1-4 für zwei Basset-hörner oder Klarinetten und Fagott</u>.
      K. Anh. 229. Bearbeitet für Streichinstrumente von Paul Klengel. Für 2
      Violinen und Viola. Leipzig: Breitkopf & Härtel, 1926. (separate
      parts). (M353 M939.1-4K)
   j. <u>Divertimento No. 3, B-dur (K. Anh. 229)</u>. Für Flöte, Klarinette und
      Fagott. ed. Günther Weigelt. Leipzig: F.E.C. Leuckart, 1936. (separate
      parts). (M359 M939D.3)
   k. <u>Adagio K. 411 (440a)</u>, arr. for clarinet quintet. New York: Mercury Music
      Co., 1946. (score and separate parts). (M559 M939A K440a)

<u>Records</u>

<u>Title</u>	<u>Music</u>	<u>Recording</u>	<u>Call No.</u>

The abbreviation "W" refers to <u>The Chamber Music of Mozart</u>, ed. Wier (<u>M</u> 1)

I. String Instruments
  A. Quartets

Title	Music	Recording	Call No.
1. K. 80 (G), 155 (D), 156 (G), 157 (C)		Vox 8510 (Barchet)	
2. K. 155 (D)		Lon 665 (Italiano)	
3. K. 158 (F), 159 (B-flat), 160 (E-flat)		Vox 8690 (Barchet)	
4. K. 168 (F)		Lon 658 (Griller)	
5. K. 171 (d)		Vox 6420 (Loewenguth)	
6. K. 387, 421, 428, 458, 464, 465		Col 187 (Budapest)	
7. K. 387 (G).	W, 9	Col 4726 (Budapest) All 26 (Loewenguth)	
8. K. 421 (d)	W, 18	Col 4726 (Budapest)	

9. K. 428 (E-flat)   W, 24   Col 4727 (Budapest)

10. K.458 (B-flat)   W, 32   Col 4727 (Budapest)

11. K. 464 (A)   W, 40   Col 4728 (Budapest)

12. K. 465 (C)   W, 49   Col 4728 (Budapest)

13. K. 499 (D)   W, 58   West 5356 (Barylli)
                                          Phil 105 (Stuyvesant)
                                          Mer 10133 (Roth)

14. K. 575 (D)   W, 68   West 5356 (Barylli)
                                          Phil 105 (Stuyvesant)
                                          Mer 10133 (Roth)

15. K. 589 (B-flat)   W, 76   West 5265 (Barylli)
                                          Vox 8260 (Barchet)

16. K. 590 (F)   W, 83   West 5092 (Amadeus)
                                          Lon 665 (Italiano)

B. Quintets
17. K. 174 (B-flat)   CH 1185 (Pascal)

18. K. 406 (c)   W, 126   Col 4143 (Budapest)
                                          CH 1186 (Pascal)

19. K. 515 (C)   W, 135   Col 4034 (Budapest)
                                          CH 1185 (Pascal)

20. K. 516 (g)   W, 150   Col 4469 (Budapest)
                                          CH 1186 (Pascal)

21. K. 593 (D),   W, 162   CH 1187 (Pascal)
                                          Col 4143 (Budapest)

22. K. 614 (E-flat)   W, 174   Col 4469 (Budapest)
                                          West 5007 (Vienna)
                                          CH 1187 (Pascal)

II. Piano and Other Instruments
     A. Trios for piano, violin, cello
23. K. 254   W, 278   Vox 8493 (Trio di Bolzano)
    K. 496   W, 271
    K. 502   W, 245
    K. 542   W, 259
    K. 548   W, 253
    K. 564   W, 266

24. K. 496, 502   West 5242 (Fournier)

25. K. 542, 548   West 5267 (Janigro)

26. K. 564, 254   West 5284 (Badura-Skoda)

27. K. 502, 542   All 3014 (Boston)

     B. Trios for piano, viola, clarinet
28. K. 498 (E-flat)   W, 239   Lyr 9 (Lifshey, Brody,
                                          Arnold)

                                    Vox 8493 (Trio di Bolzano)

   C. Piano quartets (with strings)
29. K. 478 (g)   W, 93   Col 4080 (Szell, Budapest) L
                                             Lon 679 (Curzon, Amadeus)

30. K. 493 (E-flat)   W, 102   Col 4080 (Szell, Budapest)
                                             Lon 679 (Curzon, Amadeus)

   D. Piano quintet (with winds)
31. K. 452 (E-flat)   Col 4834 (Serkin)
                                             West 5007 (Raupenstauch)

III. String and Wind Instruments
   A. Quartets for flute and strings
32. K. 285 (D), 285b (C), 298 (A) W, 112   Oxford 101 (J. Baker)

33. K. 285   W, 115   West 5022 (Reznicek)

   B. Quartet for oboe and strings
34. K. 370 (F)   W, 119   Col 4566 (Tabuteau)
                                             All 62 (Gomberg)
                                             West 5022 (Kamesch)

   C. Quintet for horn and strings
35. K. 407 (E-flat)   W, 205   All 62 (Barrows)

   D. Quintet for clarinet and strings
36. K. 581 (A)   W, 194   Lon 573 (de Bavier)
                                             Col 4483 (Goodman)

LUDWIG VAN BEETHOVEN (1770 - 1827)

I. Life

1770	Born at Bonn-on-Rhine, December 16.
1775	Lessons on clavier and violin from father, a singer in Electoral choir in Bonn, and local teachers. Father hoped to develop an infant prodigy like Mozart.
1778	Gave first concert in Cologne; advertised as "six years old."
1781	Lessons with Christian G. Neefe; began to compose. Became substitute organist for Neefe at the Electoral Chapel (1782).
1783	Appointed harpsichord and viola player in court orchestra and accompanist at the theatre (without salary); opportunity to learn new music in various fields.
1784	Appointed assistant court organist (with salary) in addition to other duties. Studied violin with Franz Ries (1785).
1787	Visited Vienna; played for Mozart and received a few lessons. His mother's death left Beethoven to take care of his two brothers and an intemperate father. Met Haydn on his visit to Bonn (1790).
1792	Haydn's second visit to Bonn. Beethoven accepted by Haydn as a pupil; later sent to Vienna by the Elector to study with Haydn. Father died; many personal difficulties arose. Success as a piano virtuoso and teacher.
1794	Began lessons with Albrechtsberger when Haydn went to London. Learned vocal style from Salieri, an opera composer; quartet-writing from Förster. Soon became his own teacher. Success as a composer.
1798	First signs of deafness appeared. By 1801 he realized that his career as a performer would soon be over.
1803-15	Composed many of his great works; symphonies (nos. 3-8), sonatas, chamber music, etc. Many unsuccessful love affairs.
1816-20	Trouble over his nephew Karl. Few works composed between 1816-18; after that a new style appeared.
1827	Died March 26; buried in Central Friedhof, Vienna, beside Haydn, Mozart, Gluck, Schubert, Wolf.

II. Catalogue of Chamber Music (arrangements are not included).

    A. String Instruments
        1. Quartets
           a. 17 for 2 violins, viola, cello (including "Grosse Fuge").
           b. 1 string quartet arranged (1802) from the Piano Sonata in E, Op. 14, No. 1 (1799).
        2. Trios
           a. 5 for violin, viola, cello.
        3. Quintets
           a. 1 for 2 violins, 2 violas, cello.

        b. 1 fugue for 2 violins, 2 violas, cello.
- B. Piano with other instruments
  1. Sonatas
     a. 10 for piano, violin.
     b. 5 for piano, cello.
     c. 1 for piano, horn
  2. Trios
     a. 8 for piano, violin, cello.
     b. 1 for piano, clarinet, cello.
     c. 1 for piano, flute, bassoon.
  3. Quartets
     a. 3 for piano, violin, viola, cello.
  4. Quintet
     a. 1 for piano, oboe, clarinet, bassoon, horn (also for piano quartet).
- C. String with wind instruments
  1. Trios
     a. Serenade for flute, violin, viola.
  2. Sextet
     a. 1 for 2 violins, viola, cello, 2 horns.
  3. Septet
     a. 1 for violin, viola, clarinet, cello, bassoon, horn, double-bass.
- D. Wind Instruments
  1. Duos
     a. 3 for clarinet, bassoon.
  2. Trios
     a. 1 for 2 oboes, English horn.
  3. Quartets
     a. 3 _Equale_ for 4 trombones.
  4. Sextet
     a. 1 for 2 clarinets, 2 horns, 2 bassoons.
  5. Octet
     a. 1 for 2 oboes, 2 clarinets, 2 horns, 2 bassoons.
     b. _Rondino_ for 2 oboes, 2 clarinets, 2 bassoons, 2 horns.

III. Chamber Music

- A. Beethoven's compositions are usually divided into three periods:
  1. 1785-1800: influence of the music of Haydn, Mozart, Johann Schobert, Mannheim School. "Period of imitation."
  2. 1800-16: the human, mature composer. "Period of externalization."
  3. 1816-27: development of a new style, high above material considerations. "Period of reflection."
- B. Chamber music was composed throughout his life. Includes about fifty works, not including arrangements. Earliest works were three quartets for piano and strings, composed in Bonn, 1785. His last work was a quartet movement.
  1. Characteristic devices began to appear in compositions of the early Vienna period (1792-1800); themes constructed out of repetitions of a short rhythmic motive; elaborate codas; principle of thematic development; expansion of harmonic scheme; third relationships; sudden modulations.
  2. After 1800 his works generally became more powerful, with greater contrasts in texture and themes and even more harmonic freedom.
  3. In his last period (1816-27) his music became sublimated, and new and unusual forms, style and modes of expression appeared.

IV. String Quartets, First Period (1798-1801).

- A. 6 Quartets Op. 18: No. 1 (F), No. 2 (G), No. 3 (D), No. 4 (c), No. 5 (A), No. 6 (B-flat).

1. Dedicated to Prince von Lobkowitz, one of Beethoven's patrons. Published in sets of three by Tranquillo Mollo in 1801. Chronological order according to composition: No. 3, No. 1, No. 2, No. 5, No. 6, No. 4. First Symphony completed in 1799.
2. First violin often given special emphasis; second violin and viola are subordinated; the cello provides a harmonic bass.
   a. Short, simple, diatonic, rhythmic motives are usually basis for first movements.
   b. Slow movements are generally ornate; frequently longer than with Haydn or Mozart; themes in regular phtases.
   c. Third movements are usually very fast.
   d. Texture is generally more harmonic than contrapuntal; all four instruments rarely have separate contrapuntal lines. Quartets are not related, but all show mastery of form, new techniques, consistent style. There are many sudden contrasts in rhythm and dynamics.

B. Op. 18, No. 1 (F)
   1. Allegro con brio (F).
      a. Shows Beethoven's skill at working out a rhythmic motive, which appears over 100 times in 303 measures. Introduced in unison; treated in imitation, as sequence, as an accompanied melody, and contrapuntally.
      b. Sonata-form. Development (meas. 115-178) uses the theme in imitation and in various keys. Recapitulation (meas. 179-313).
   2. Adagio affettuoso ed appassionato (d).
      a. Sonata-form: Exposition (meas. 1-45); second theme (meas. 26); Development (meas. 46-62); Recapitulation (meas. 63-95); Coda (meas. 96-110).
   3. Scherzo and Trio: Allegro molto (F).
      a. A fast Minuet in Haydn style. Melody modulates to dominant; this is repeated and then leads to a contrasting section (meas. 11-36) modulating through A-flat, f, D-flat, f, ending on dominant harmony. It then returns to the principal theme; second part is much longer than in the usual Scherzo form.
      b. Trio is built on contrast of two themes, (1) a leaping octave passage in unison, (2) a running scale passage for the first violin.
   4. Allegro (F).
      a. Sonata-Rondo form. A (meas. 1-42)-B (meas. 43-90)-A(meas. 91-102)-Development (meas. 103-234)-A (meas. 235-278)-B (meas. 279-326)-A and Coda (meas. 327-381).

C. Op. 18, No. 2 (G).
   1. Allegro (G).
      a. Begins immediately with the principal theme, which consists of three short motives. Sectional treatment in conversational style. Exposition (meas. 1-81), second theme (meas. 36); Development (meas. 82-144); Recapitulation (meas. 145-232); Coda (meas. 233-248).
   2. Adagio Cantabile (C).
      a. Ternary song form. The cantabile melody of twenty six measures is followed by an Allegro (F) (meas. 27-58), then a return to the first section with rich ornamentation (meas. 59-86).
   3. Scherzo: Allegro (G).
      a. Lively eight-measure melody built on a rising four-note motive.
   4. Allegro molto quasi Presto (G).
      a. Sonata-form. The first theme built on a chordal figure D-G-B, announced by the cello. Development (meas. 82-144); Recapitulation (meas. 145-232); Coda (meas. 233-248).

D. Op. 18, No. 3 (D). First quartet of Op. 18 to be written.
   1. Allegro (D).
      a. Shows the influence for Haydn and Mozart. First theme is a treatment in free imitation of the opening phrases. Second theme (meas. 51) introduces a new rhythm. Development (meas. 108-158) section

short; begins like the Exposition, but in minor.
2. Andante con moto (B-flat).
    a. Begins with first and second violins on fourth string. Slow move-
       ment, with its extended development, is the central point of the
       whole quartet.
3. Scherzo and Trio: Allegro (D).
    a. An unusual movement. No literal repetition of the "Maggiore"
       section after the Trio. The section starts out as usual and is
       then extended. The two violins are transferred to a higher re-
       gister and a different key.
4. Presto (D).
    a. Sonata-form. Vigorous gigue-like rhythm throughout. Second theme
       (meas. 56); Development (meas. 114-210); Recapitulation (meas. 210).
E. Op. 18, No. 4 (c).
1. Allegro ma non troppo (c).
    a. Begins with a soft, expressive melody. The transition (meas. 13-
       33) begins with a crash of alternate tonic and dominant chords,
       leading to a strenuous passage on a dominant pedal. Entrance of
       the second theme is delayed until measure 34.
2. Scherzo: Andante scherzoso (C).
    a. Sonata-form with fugal expositions. Second theme is used in canon-
       ic imitation. Not a typical scherzo. Principal section (meas. 1-
       42); subsidiary section (meas. 43-67); closing section (meas. 67-
       82); Development (meas. 83-145).
3. Menuetto: Allegretto (c).
    a. First theme, a rising melody, makes use of syncopation.
4. Allegro: Prestissimo (c).
    a. Rondo form: A-B-A-C-A-B-A. Main idea and both episodes are pre-
       sented as separate sections, enclosed within double bars. This
       quartet is more symphonic than any of the others in Op. 18.
F. Op. 18, No. 5 (A).
1. Allegro (A).
    a. Principal section (meas. 1-24); subsidiary section (meas. 25-55);
       closing section (meas. 55-79). First phrase of theme is the ascend-
       ing scale of A. Design and development suggest influence of Mozart.
2. Menuetto (A).
    a. Begins with a violin melody, taken up later by viola. Trio is in
       binary form.
3. Andante cantabile (D).
    a. Variation form in the style of Mozart. Five variations, the last
       one leading to the Coda.
4. Allegro (A).
    a. Sonata-form. A motive is the basic idea. Second theme is a con-
       trasting slow chordal passage (meas. 36). Closing section (meas.
       71-94). Recapitulation begins in measure 168; Coda (meas. 264).
G. Op. 18, No. 6 (B-flat).
1. Allegro con brio (B-flat).
    a. A dialogue between the first violin and cello; viola and second
       violin accompany. Second idea enters at measure 44. Development
       section from measure 92-152.
2. Adagio ma non troppo (E-flat).
    a. Extended and elaborated ternary song form with Coda in tonic.
3. Scherzo : Allegro (B-flat).
    a. Remarkable use of syncopation. One of most original movements of
       Op. 18. Trio is in style of Haydn; first violin prominent.
4. Adagio ("La Malinconia"):- Allegretto (B-flat).
    a. Allegretto section in rondo form: A (meas. 45-76) - B (meas. 77-
       104) - A^1 (meas. 105-149) - B^1 (meas. 150-181) - A^2 (meas. 182-
       194) - C (meas. 195-211) - A^3 with a short development and Coda
       (meas. 212-296).

V. String Quartets, Second Period (1806-10).

   A. Quartets Op. 59: No. 1 (F), No. 2 (e), No. 3 (C); Op. 74 (E-flat); Op. 95
      (f).
     1. Quartets of the second period (1806-10) are written with complete tech-
        nical mastery. Style shows frequent expressive contrasts; use of dia-
        logue between instruments; alternation of rhythmic motives; symphonic
        tendencies in final movements; emphasis of main musical idea; diatonic
        themes; extensive use of thematic development; more use of counter-
        point; more virtuoso writing for instruments; higher organization of
        form; extensive use of sonata-form which is expanded and given freer
        treatment.
        a. Op. 59, known as the "Rasoumovsky Quartets," were commissioned by
           the Russian Count, Rasoumovsky. They are related by the use of
           Russian folk songs (Nos. 1, 2) and inner content.
   B. Op. 59, No. 1 (F) (1806)
     1. Allegro (F).
        a. Two motives, announced by cello in first four measures, build up
           the first movement. Contrapuntal treatment is used in the Develop-
           ment.
     2. Allegretto vivace e sempre scherzando (B-flat).
        a. Sonata-form. Begins with dialogue between the cello and second
           violin. First motive is a rhythmic figure on one note, which
           recurs throughout. Dynamics range from p to sudden ff; melodic
           sections break off into others with great leaps; unexpected modu-
           lations; sudden contrasts.
     3. Adagio molto e mesto (f).
        a. Sonata-form, but second theme (meas. 24) is modified and elaborated
           on its return.
     4. Thème Russe: Allegro (F).
        a. Sonata-form with Rondo characteristics. No break between third and
           fourth movements. Begins in F, modulates to d, then to C, introduc-
           ing the second theme (meas. 45). Russian melody enters in c. De-
           velopment section uses thematic development (meas. 100-178).
   C. Op. 59, No. 2 (c).
     1. Allegro (c).
        a. Begins with tonic and dominant chords, followed by a measure rest;
           short principal theme of Op. 18 type then enters. Development
           section uses opening chords as underlying motive. Modulations in
           the Development from E-flat to b, G, A-flat, resolving in C.
     2. Molto Adagio (E).
        a. Sonata-form (second theme, meas. 27). Begins with chorale-like
           section based on two phrases; after repetition in lower register, a
           triplet figure appears which continues throughout the movement.
           Chorale then progresses from B to D, then changes quickly to minor
           and a modulation is made to B-flat. Agitated triplet figure con-
           tinues as before.
        b. Chorale passage comes back and begins the Development section;
           modulates by means of the dominant of A, goes from major to minor,
           then to E. Chorale theme again enters in all four instruments.
           Dynamics and register are gradually lowered and the movement ends
           softly on E.
     3. Allegretto (c). Scherzo.
        a. Form: A-A-B-B-C-A-B. Unusual rhythmic pattern in the first section;
           triple meter with the accent on the second beat, a dotted quarter
           note.
        b. Second section is in quieter mood in g; modulates to a, then F
           (using the accented second-beat rhythmic pattern), and e. "Mag-
           giore" section is based on a Russian folk tune. Fugato section
           uses the melody canonically and sometimes as an accompanied melody.

4. Finale: Presto (e).
  a. Rondo form: A (meas. 1-69) - B (meas. 70-106) - A^1 (meas. 107-145) - Development (meas. 146-215) - B^1 (meas. 216-274) - A^2 and Coda (meas. 275-409). Begins with C chord in all instruments. First violin carries the melody, with lower strings playing a rhythmical chordal accompaniment. Modulation to e after seven measures with a quick return to C. "Più presto" begins in e and established the fundamental tonality. Much rhythmic movement and massive chordal writing in the closing measures.

D. Op. 59, No. 3 (C).
  1. Andante con moto - Allegro vivace (C).
    a. First use in Beethoven's quartets of a slow opening section. Introduction is in triple meter with shifting harmonies, which finally establish the key of the Allegro (C).
    b. First violin opens the Allegro and introduces the principal theme in a typical rhythmic pattern. This is repeated in d and ends on the dominant of F, modulating back to C. Second theme is also introduced by the first violin (meas. 77). Imitation is freely used in passages which follow. Development leads to E-flat and the first theme reappears. The keys passed through are: F, c, F, finally to C. Principal theme then begins the third section of the movement.
  2. Andante con moto quasi Allegretto (a).
    a. Sonata-form (second theme, meas. 42). The long melodic line is introduced by the first violin, accompanied by pizzicato cello, which continues without accent or break. Contrary motion between strings is prominent in the following passage. After the second repeated sect section, louder dynamics and a higher register are used for contrast. Keys used in the Development are A, d, E-flat. First theme, now modified, comes in after the development in E.
  3. Menuetto: Grazioso (C).
    a. Some elements of sonata-form. Divided into two sections, the first not repeated. First section is chordal and rhythmic; the upper three instruments play in the same note values. Second section is entirely different; first violin plays a phrase based on the principal motive, accompanied by other instruments. Phrase introduced by the first violin is treated in imitation.
    b. Trio begins with an arpeggiated figure based on the F triad. Divided into two sections: first ends in C; second begins in A without preparation and then becomes the dominant of e, this going to F.
  4. Allegro molto (C).
    a. Sonata-form with fugal principal section. Climax of Op. 59 and an unusually outstanding movement. Fugal style; the subject, which is ten measures long, is introduced by the viola, followed by the second violin, cello, first violin. Subject is used in imitation between the instruments, leading to an episode in E-flat. Keys which follow are f, D-flat, c-sharp; throughout this section the principal subject is introduced in many modified versions.
    b. Modulation from c-sharp to d; the section which follows is one of great tension and dramatic power. First violin then takes a fragment of the opening subject and, with the sforzando chordal accompaniment, builds a powerful climax.
    c. A delay follows on the dominant of C, then the fugal treatment of the subject begins again. Instruments enter as in the Exposition, only this time a new countersubject is used. Material is used with some modification leading to the Coda. The subject is now heard in contrary motion, in short statements.

E. Op. 74 (E-flat) (1800). Op. 74 and Op. 95 transitional in style.

1. Poco Adagio - Allegro (E-flat).
   a. Introduction of twenty-four measures. Downward leap a prominent
      figure, occurring nine times. Effective modulatory passages.
   b. Allegro is linked to the introduction by a series of energetic
      chords. Principal theme enters (meas. 27). Pizzicato harp-like
      accompaniment used in measures 35, 125, 153, 221, 251. Development
      is in three sections, built on the principal theme and a thematic
      figure.
2. Adagio ma non troppo (A-flat).
   a. Rondo form: A-B-A-C-A-Coda. Long, unbroken melody, introduced by
      the first violin; less ornamental than Op. 18. B section comes in
      (meas. 25) eithout any transition, leading to the tonic minor;
      about thirty-six measures of modulatory writing follows.
   b. A section returns (meas. 64) with a new accompaniment in the inner
      parts, ending on A-flat. C section (meas. 87). First violin
      states the principal theme for the third time (meas. 115), modified
      in its further restatement. Coda (meas. 139-169); A and B themes
      appear.
3. Presto (c).
   a. Scherzo form with repeated Trio. Comparable to the Allegro of the
      Fifth Symphony; uses same rhythmic figure. Fast scherzo-like move-
      ment in ABA form with repeated Trio. After opening in c, the music
      goes through several modulations leading into a new section in g.
      Modulations to the dominant of F, then f, c, ending abruptly in C.
4. Allegretto con variatione (E-flat).
   a. Variation form with six variations, some divided into two sections.
      Other "partial" variations enter in the Coda.
F. Op. 95 (f) (1810). "Quartet Serioso."
   1. Allegro con brio (f).
      a. Begins with a strong unison passage announcing the first half of
         the principal theme. Second half of the first theme is strongly
         rhythmical. Second theme (meas. 24) is in D-flat; suggests figures
         and rhythms of the first theme. Many unprepared modulations and
         chromatic transitions: G-flat, F, D-flat, A-flat, A, D-flat, D,
         D-flat, A-flat, F. Development treats the principal theme in imita-
         tion, then exploits the second half of the theme. Recapitulation
         (meas. 83) discards the second half of the theme. Second theme re-
         appears ih D-flat and moves to F. Rhythmic motive is persistently
         used in the Coda (meas. 129).
   2. Allegretto ma non troppo (D).
      a. Ternary song form, or Aria form in five sections. Opens with a
         slow downward scale passage in the cello of four measures length.
         First violin enters at the fifth measure with a lonf melody made up
         of several phrases. Harmonic feeling shifts between D and g.
         Viola announces a theme (meas. 34) which is developed fugally.
         Single notes of the cello recur and the section ends on the domi-
         nant of D (meas. 76). Fugato section is repeated. Recapitulation
         of Section I begins in measure 112. Fugato theme enters abruptly
         in the viola (meas. 144). Second phrase of the first melody (meas.
         153) enters in the cello. The work ends on a diminished seventh
         with the introductory idea.
   3. Allegro assai vivace, ma serioso (f).
      a. Fast, highly rhythmical Scherzo movement in A-B-A-B-A form; uses
         contrapuntal devices.
      b. Trio begins (meas. 40) after the first section (meas. 1-39) has
         been repeated. Chordal, chorale-like melody in the three lower
         strings is accompanied by the first violin in a harp-like figure.
         The cello takes the melody and modulations fo through D then to b.
      c. First Recapitulation of Scherzo (meas. 103). Trio (meas. 145) is
         in D instead of G-flat. Modulation through G, c, f. Scherzo re-
         turns in f (meas. 183).

   4. **Larghetto expressivo - Allegretto agitato (f-F).**
       a. Short, expressive, romantic introduction moves wuickly to the agitated Allegretto in Rondo-Sonata form. First theme is composed of two motives and a concluding phrase. Second theme (intermediate section) enters in the second violin (meas. 44). Imitation between viola and cello.
       b. The first section returns, followed by a short Development; second motive of the first theme is used in close imitation. The second theme (intermediate section) enters in f (meas. 94). First section returns (meas. 95); first theme is taken by the first violin, accompanied by lower strings. Coda (meas. 133) in F introduces a new theme in the first violin.

IV. **String Quartets, Third Period (1824-26):** Op. 127 (E-flat); Op. 132 (a); Op. 130 (B-flat); Op. 133 ("Grosse Fuge"); Op. 131 (c-sharp); Op. 135 (F).

   A. Three Quartets (Op. 127, 132, 130) were commissioned by Prince Galitzin, a wealthy Russian amateur cellist. Third Period quartets were not composed in the order in which they are numbered, but as given above.
   B. Style shows continuous organic development; extended melodic lines; use of tones foreign to key; equal interest among instruments; increased polyphonic complexity; all parts independent; complex part-writing; powerful syncopation; tendency to use extremely unrelated keys; adaptation of material; use of more than four parts; changing tempos; slow opening sections (except Op. 135).
   C. **Op. 127 (E-flat) (1824).**
       1. **Maestoso: Allegro (E-flat).**
           a. Movement is mostly contrapuntal; the only homophonic passages are in the maestoso sections, the two bridge cadences, the two appearances of the second theme. Movement opens with a four-measure melody reminiscent of a Bach subject. Development begins with the second Allegro (meas. 81-166); includes two statements of the Maestoso section. Coda is from leasure 241 to end.
       2. **Adagio, ma non troppo (A-flat).**
           a. Simple harmonization of a diatonic scale-wise melody followed by five variations. One of Beethoven's finest movements.
       3. **Scherzando vivace (E-flat).**
           a. Theme is a four-note staccato group; used in all possible ways. Many sudden changes of dynamics and tempo.
       4. **Finale (E-flat).**
           a. Opens with a four-measure Introduction; folk-like theme is then announced. Arpeggio motive is introduced; appears in all instruments at different times.
           b. Development is introduced after a recurrence of the four-measure introduction. Second theme enters in C, then in c; then is used in canon. At the Allegro commodo (6/8), Beethoven subtly and slowly moves to E-flat; harmonies then change oftener, and finally reach the tonic.
   D. **Op. 130 (B-flat) (1825-26).**
       1. **Adagio ma non troppo: Allegro (B-flat).**
           a. Adagio is an introduction of fourteen measures. Development section uses some of this material. At the Allegro, two figures appear, one in sixteenth notes introduced by the first violin, the other in quarter notes introduced by the second violin. These aappear frequently in the following measures.
           b. Development begins at measure 94 in the key of G-flat. D is reached by enharmonic change of g-flat to f-sharp. These is one measure of Allegro, three measures of Adagio, again - Allegro, Adagio, and finally Allegro, this time continuing with the quarter-note figure in the first violin and cello. Recapitulation (meas. 132-213). Short Adagios and Allegros reappear in Coda (meas. 214).

2. Presto: Scherzo (b-flat).
    a. First section is divided into two parts; each is repeated, ending
        in B-flat. Trio (meas. 17-63) is in two parts, each repeated,
        followed by a transitory passage leading to a Recapitulation of
        the Scherzo. First violin uses a modified principal theme in a
        sequential manner, accompanied by lower instruments. This theme
        appears continuously until the scale passages leading to the rit-
        ardando section; all instruments are in dotted half rhythm.
    b. A short solo passage for first violin appears at the return of
        "L'istesso tempo," followed by a forte unison of all instruments
        on a three-note figure. This passage is used twice again, differ-
        ently each time. First section returns with the melody modified
        and the use of imitation. Coda (meas. 96) introduces principal
        theme in mirror, with viola reiterating it in normal position.
3. Andante con moto, ma non troppo (D-flat).
    a. Sonata-form: Exposition (meas. 1-25), Development (meas. 29-37),
        Recapitulation (meas. 38-65). Movement begins in the key of B-
        flat. The first theme is introduced by the viola in measure 3 and
        taken by the first violin an octave higher in measure 5. Inter-
        change of melodic material is followed by free imitation (meas. 20).
    b. Cantabile section, with the melody in the first violin (meas. 26)
        is repeated in simplified form. The coda begins at measure 66 with
        the appearance of a pizzicato accompaniment in the lower strings;
        modulatory passages and unprepared chords lead to a novel conclu-
        sion on D-flat.
4. Alla danza tedesca: Allegro assai (G).
    a. Ternary song form in the style of a German dance; originally writ-
        ten for Op. 132. Main section (meas. 1-24) and Trio (meas. 25-80),
        with customary repetitions, recall early type of Scherzo. Recapi-
        tulation (meas. 81-128) is followed by the Coda (meas. 129). Germ
        of the movement is found in the first four measures.
5. Cavatina: Adagio molto expressivo (E-flat).
    a. Long, expressive melodic phrase. First period is nine measures
        long, repeated but slightly modified and shortened. Second theme
        enters at measure 23 in the second violin; freely imitated by first
        violin. Middle section (meas. 40-49); Recapitulation (meas. 50-
        66).
6. Finale : Allegro (B-flat).
    a. Sonata-Rondo form: A-B-C-Development-Recapitulation-D-A-Coda. In
        its original form this work concluded with the "Grosse Fuge," but
        owing to its extreme length it was replaced in 1825 by this move-
        ment and the fugue was published separately as Op. 133.
    b. This finale was Beethoven's last work. It opens with the solo
        viola playing an octave accompaniment figure; main theme is in the
        first violin. Entire movement is devoted to the working out of
        this material; mirroring, imitation and "passing around" of themes.
        B section (meas. 67-108) followed by C section (meas. 109-161).
    c. Development begins at measure 162, Recapitulation at measure 223,
        D section at measure 253, final A section at measure 430.
E. Op. 131 (c-sharp) (1826). (Seven movements played without interruption).
    1. Adagio ma non troppo e molto expressivo (c-sharp).
        a. Principal theme, introduced by the first violin, is four measures
            long. It is treated in fugal style with entrances by other instru-
            ments every four measures. After the final entrance of the Exposi-
            tion in the cello, the contrapuntal writing becomes free. Imita-
            tion between the first violin and cello, and the second violin and
            viola (meas. 21). Much contrapuntal writing follows, with new imi-
            tations. Suggestions of Parsifal in measures 63-66. First violin
            takes the subject from the viola (meas. 99); this is followed by
            the augmentation of the subject by the cello (meas. 100). Modula-
            tion to tonic, c-sharp.

2. Allegro molto vivace (D).
    a. A bright homophonic movement contrasted with a somber first move-
        ment. First violin has the theme, accompanied by sustained pass-
        ages in the other instruments. Viola takes the theme (meas. 9),
        then first violin. Second theme in measure 24. Music becomes
        more polyphonic with the "working out" of the rhythmic figuration;
        unusual harmonic progression (meas. 66-67). Return of the princi-
        pal themes, leading without stop to the next section.
3. Allegro moderato: Adagio (b).
    a. A short recitative-like introduction of eleven measures leads to
        a theme and variations.
4. Andante ma non troppo e molto cantabile (A, Coda in C).
    a. Theme and seven variations with an extended Coda. Theme is thirty-
        two measures long, divided between the two violins. Consists of
        two eight-measure sections, each repeated.
    b. Variation I.
        1) Second violin approximates the theme in different rhythm; first
            violin has falling phrases in sixteenths. At the repetition,
            the cello has the falling phrases.
    c. Variation II (Più mosso).
        1) First half of the theme is used in a duet between the violin and
            cello. The second half of the theme is used in a modified ver-
            sion. The cello takes the second half at the repetition.
    d. Variation III (Andante moderato e lusinghiero).
        1) Begins with a canon at the second between the viola and cello,
            which is repeated by the violins. Second section (meas. 113)
            starts with another canon, again between viola and cello. It is
            later joined by the cviolins at the repeat.
    e. Variation IV (Adagio).
        1) Little similarity between this variation and the theme. Motive
            in measure 3 is used. Passages are accentuated by pizzicato
            notes; violins have a duet in thirds, sixths, octaves.
    f. Variation V (Allegretto).
        1) Instruments begin with double stops. The music is very re-
            strained. based on the harmony of the theme.
    g. Variation VI (Adagio, ma non troppo e semplice).
        1) Begins with a chordal pattern, which is later used an octave
            higher (meas. 195). Solo ascending scale passage in the first
            violin (meas. 220) is later given to viola, cello, second
            violin. First violin takes the scale passage in a descending
            pattern, leading eventually to Variation VII.
    h. Variation VII.
        1) Incomplete and in recitative style.
    i. Coda (Allegretto) (C).
        1) Beginning of the principal theme is stated in country-dance
            style. Trills are used throughout. There is a display of vir-
            tuosity before the sudden close of the movement.
5. Presto: Scherzo (E).
    a. First entrance by cello is only one measure long, followed by the
        full measure rest. Short development of the first two measures of
        the theme. Theme in g-sharp, returning quickly to original key.
        This is repeated, and the "B" theme is introduced (meas. 69); key
        changes to A. Trio begins (meas. 110) with the rhythm in four-
        measure phrases. A new theme begins at measure 141. Return to
        "A" then "B" theme; reference to "C" theme. First use of ponti-
        cello bowing (close to the bridge) in a quartet (meas. 470).
6. Adagio quasi un poco andante (g-sharp).
    a. Viola introduces first theme, which is then taken over by the
        first violin. Theme is heard throughout this short movement,
        which leads directly to the Finale.

      7. Allegro (c-sharp).
          a. Sonata-form. Theme is a group made up of three themes, all of
which are developed. "A(1)" appears in measure 2, "A(2)" in measures 5-8, "A(3)" in measure 21 (first violin). Themes are treated
contrapuntally in the sections which follow. Part of the fugue
theme of the first movement appears in measures 30-31. Coda uses
melody made up of the three themes, treated in a new way.

F. Op. 132 (a) (1824-25).
    1. Assai sostenuto: Allegro (a).
        a. Cello introduces "A" theme in first and second measures, mirrored
by viola in measures 3 and 4. This theme appears in various forms
in Quartets Op. 132 (a), Op. 133 ("Grosse Fuge"), Op. 131 (c-
sharp). First theme is suggested by the cello (meas. 11) and
played completely by the first violin (meas. 13, then repeated by
the cello and continued by the viola. Second theme enters in
measure 48.
        b. Development begins at measure 75 with the entrance of cello stating
"A" theme. Recapitulation (meas. 119) begins in the key of e and
follows the Exposition fairly closely. The Coda (meas. 189) follows, passing through a, A, and ending with a crescendo in a.
    2. Allegro ma non tanto (A).
        a. Scherzo and Trio with a "da capo" at the end of the middle section.
Restrained in mood. Thematic material is found in measures 5 and
6. Main theme in the first violin, "B" theme in the second violin.
Movement opens with "B" theme in octaves in all four instruments.
The two themes are found in all but five measures of the main
section. Trio begins at measure 120, followed by the da capo.
    3. Molto Adagio: Andante.
        a. "Holy Song of Thanksgiving to the Divinity by a Convalescent, in
the Lydian Mode." Form: A-B-A varied-B-A varied-Coda. Adagio
section uses a chorale-like tune of five phrases in the Lydian
mode. Fragment found in the opening three measures is used in
later sections. Andante section ("the invalid feels new strength")
(meas. 31) in D moves vigorously and in contrast to the first
section. Theme of this section is in the second violin; repeated
in measure 39; rest of the section is less vigorous and it ends
pianissimo. Adagio returns (meas. 84), and the first violin has
the chorale tune an octave higher; less imitation, but more syncopation, especially in the second violin and cello. Andante reappears (meas. 115) almost as before, except that the violin has
the theme, followed later by the second violin. In the third
appearance of the Adagio (meas. 168), the first phrase of the
chorale tune is used; imitation at different intervals, and at
different parts of the measure.
    4. Alla marcia, assai vivace (A).
        a. First section consists of eight measures repeated. A second sec-
      6   tion (meas. 9-14) and recapitulation of first section follows, also
repeated. A Recitative, Più Allegro, enters (meas. 25); first
violin has a recitative passage, accompanied by tremolo strings;
followed by a solo for first violin (Presto), leading directly to
Finale.
    5. Allegro appassionato (a).
        a. Rondo form: A-B-A-C-A-B-A. Main theme is introduced by the first
violin; repeated an octave higher soon after. "B" section (meas.
52-59). After the fourth appearance of the main melody, a Coda
section in A introduces two new themes. The first is stated by
the cello in high register and repeated by the violins in octaves.

G. Op. 133, "Grosse Fuge" (B-flat) (1825).
    1. Originally written as the last movement of Quartet Op. 130. It begins
in g; main theme is asserted by the four instruments (meas. 2-10).
Main theme "A", which is the basic motive used in Op. 132, appears in

various ways in measures 1-10 (g), 11-16 (to F), 17-25 (F), 26-30
(B-flat). Called "Overtura" in the original manuscript.

2. Section I (meas. 30-158, B-flat to G-flat) uses a new theme "B" with
    the main theme "A" as a countersubject.

3. Section II, Meno mosso 2/4 (meas. 159-232, G-flat to B-flat), uses
    theme "B" altered.

4. Section III, Allegro molto 6/8 (meas. 233-272, B-flat), uses theme
    "A" in Scherzo style.

5. Section IV (meas. 273-413, A-flat) expands theme "A", which appears
    in diminution at measure 350.

6. Section V (meas. 414-662, E-flat) uses themes "A" and "B", and Sections
    II (meno mosso, 2/4) and III (Allegro molto, 6/8) return.

7. Section VI (meas. 663-741, B-flat), the final section, presents theme
    "A" in the tonic with "B" as a countermelody.

H. Op. 135 (F) (1826).

1. Allegretto.

    a. Built on many themes and fragmentary statements. Main theme ap-
        pears in the first measure, stated by the viola, and is repeated.
        A new idea appears, played in octaves by the violin and viola (meas.
        10). First violin introduces another theme (meas. 24). A new
        theme appears in a three-octave unison passage (meas. 46). The
        closing theme enters at measure 54.

    b. Development begins with a cello solo (meas. 62); use of triple in-
        vertible counterpoint.

    c. There is an unusual use of themes in the Recapitulation (meas. 101-
        163). Material which follows is a modified version of the main
        fragments. Coda (meas. 163) is treated similarly to the Develop-
        ment.

2. Vivace: Scherzo (F).

    a. Begins with syncopation. The main theme is in the first violin;
        repeated, after opening eight measures an octave higher by the
        second violin. Syncopation follows and the theme returns over a
        pedal "C" in the cello (meas. 25). Violin and cello exchange parts
        which opened the movement (meas. 33).

    b. The second section is repeated; leads into the Trio (meas. 67)
        which uses an ascending scale passage in F. This returns in G,
        then in A. Three lower instruments have an ostinato of fifty-one
        measures based on the cello and viola figure (meas. 142) found in
        the first measure of the Trio.

    c. First section returns and repeats; ends with a short Coda.

3. Lento assai, cantate e tranquillo (D-flat).

    a. Theme with variations. Opens with a two-measure introduction, fol-
        lowed by an eight-measure melody in the first violin, with sustain-
        ed accompaniment in the lower strings. Last measure of this phrase
        repeated by the cello and then by the first violin. First eight
        measures are varied (meas. 13-20).

    b. Middle section begins at the Più Lento in c-sharp (meas. 23). Re-
        turn to first section at Tempo I (meas. 33). Cello has the main
        theme, violin the same theme slightly modified; these two instru-
        ments are in canon, the cello following the violin. Coda (meas.
        43) is made up of fragments.

4. Grave ma non troppo: Allegro (F). "Resolution reached with diffi-
    culty."

    a. Sonata-form. The two short themes stated at the beginning, "Muss
        es sein?" and "Es muss sein!" are the motivating forces of the
        whole movement. Viola and cello state the first of the two themes
        in five of the twelve measures of the Grave. In the first four
        measures, there is close imitation, of a descending and then ascend-
        ing figure by the first violin, viola, and second violin. Allegro
        begins with the "It must be!" theme, then introduces a new theme in
        the first violin (meas. 17). This theme is used in close imitation.

first in the tonic, then in A. Second theme begins in measure 53.

    b. Development (meas. 81-173) uses the "It must be!" theme modified. A new theme, first used in the Allegro section, is again used in canon (meas. 88), with the addition of the "It must be!" theme appearing in each instrument. Music returns to "Grave" section (meas. 161-173); "Must it be?" and "It must be!" themes appear several times.

    c. Recapitulation (meas. 174-243) begins with a variation of the "It must be!" theme. Coda begins at measure 244 with a slow statement of the "It must be!" theme, which is followed by a pizzicato section leading to the close of the movement.

BIBLIOGRAPHY

Books

1. Abraham, G.   Beethoven's Second Period Quartets. London: Oxford University Press, 1942. (MT145 B41A15)

2. Bekker, P. J.   Beethoven. Tr. by M. M. Bozman. New York: E. P. Dutton, 1925. (ML410 B41B42B)

3. Burk, J. N.   The Life and Works of Beethoven. New York: Random House, 1943.

4. Carter, W.   A Study of the Third Relationship in Beethoven. ESM Thesis, 1942.

5. Dunhill, T. F.   Chamber Music - A Treatise for Students. London: Macmillan, 1925. (MT71 D91)

6. Fiske, R.   Beethoven's Last Quartets. London: Oxford University Press, 1940. (MT145 B41F31)

7. Griffin, F.   A Study of Rhythm Based on the Beethoven Op. 18 Quartets. ESM Thesis, 1945.

8. Hadow, W. H.   Beethoven's Op. 18 Quartets. London: Oxford University Press, 1926. (MT145 B41H13)

9. Herriot, E.   The Life and Times of Beethoven. Transl. by A. I. and W. J. Mitchell. New York: Macmillan, 1936. (ML410 B41H56M)

10. d'Indy, V.   Beethoven. Transl. by T. Baker. New York: G. Schirmer, 1913. (ML410 B41I42B)

11. Kalischer, A. C.   Beethoven's Letters. Transl. by J. S. Shedlock. 2 vols. New York: E. P. Dutton, 1909. (ML410 B41K)

12. Kerst, F.   Beethoven, the Man and Artist as Revealed in His Own Works. New York: B. W. Huebsch, 1905.

13. Marliave, J.   Beethoven's Quartets. Transl. by H. Andrews. London: Oxford University Press, 1928. (MT145 B41M34A)

14. Mason, D. G.   Beethoven and His Forerunners. New York: Macmillan, 1930. (ML390 M39.3)

15. Mason, D. G.   The Quartets of Beethoven. New York: Oxford University Press, 1947. (MT145 B41M398)

16. Mies, P.   Beethoven's Sketches. Transl. by Doris L. MacKinnon.
London: Oxford University Press, 1929. (ML410 B41M6)

17. Newman, E.   The Unconscious Beethoven: An Essay in Musical Psychology.
Rev. edition. New York: A. A. Knopf, 1930. (ML410 B41N55.2)

18. Nottebohm, G.   Thematisches Verzeichnis der im Druck erschienen Werke von
Ludwig van Beethoven. Leipzig: Breitkopf & Härtel, 1925 (1868).
(ML134 B41A3) This index is incomplete and out of date.

19. Rolland, R.   Beethoven. Transl. by B. C. Hull. London: Trench, 1917.
(ML410 B41R74)

20. Scott, M. M.   Beethoven. New York: E. P. Dutton, 1940. (ML410 B41S42)

21. Shepherd, A.   The String Quartets of Ludwig van Beethoven. Cleveland:
Horace Carr, The Printing Press, 1935.

22. Sullivan, J. W. N. Beethoven: His Spiritual Development. New York: A. A.
Knopf, 1927. (ML410 B41S49)

23. Thayer, A. W.   The Life of Ludwig van Beethoven. 3 vols. ed. H. E.
Krehbiel. New York: The Beethoven Association, 1921. (ML410 B41T37K)

24. Tovey, D. F.   Beethoven. ed. H. J. Foss. London, 1944.

25. Wagner, R.   Beethoven. Transl. by E. Dannreuther. London: W. Reeves,
1880. (ML410 B41W1A204D)

26. Walker, E.   Beethoven. New York & London: John Lane Co., 1907.

Periodicals

1. d'Aranyi, J.   "Beethoven's Violin Sonatas," ML 8 (1927), 191.

2. Capell, R.   "Beethoven: The Man and His Time," ML 8 (1927), 262.

3. Clarke, R.   "The Beethoven Quartets as a Player Sees Them," ML 8
(1927), 178.

4. Colles, H. C.   "Beethoven (1770-1827)," Music Bulletin 9 (1927), 77.

5. Dunhill, T. F.   "The Music of Friends: Some Thoughts on the String Quartets of Beethoven," MT 68 (1927), 113.

6. Engel, C.   "Review of Ernest Newman's 'The Unconscious Beethoven',"
MQ 13 (1927), 646.

7. Grew, S.   "Beethoven's 'Grosse Fuge'," MQ 17 (1931), 497.

8. Grew, S.   "Beethoven's 'Grosse Fuge', an analysis," ML 12 (1931),253.

9. Hadow, H.   "Beethoven's Variation Form," ML 8 (1927), 127.

10. Kolisch, R.   "Tempo and Character in Beethoven's Music," MQ 29 (1943),
169 (Part I), 291 (Part II).

11. McEwen, J. B.   "Beethoven's Third Period," ML 8 (1927), 156.

12. Oldman, C. B.   "Beethoven Bibliography," ML 8 (1927), 276.

13. Tovey, D.   "Beethoven's Forms," <u>ML</u> 8 (1927), 131.

14. Tovey, D.   "The Music Antecedents of Beethoven's Style," <u>ML</u> 25
       (1944), 63.

15. Unger, M.   "From Beethoven's Workshop," <u>MQ</u> 24 (1938), 323.

16. Walthew, R.   "The Chamber Music of Beethoven," <u>ML</u> 8 (1927), 317.

17. Watson, J. A.   "Beethoven's Debt to Mozart," <u>ML</u> 18 (1937), 248.

18. White, F.   "Some Notes (and a new book) on Beethoven's String Quar-
       tets," <u>Chesterian</u> 8 (Jan.-Feb. 1927), 122.

Music
General Editions

1. Wier, A. E.   <u>The Chamber Music of Beethoven</u>. New York: Longmans,
       Green & Co., 1940.

2. Beethoven, L. v. <u>Werke</u>. 46 vols. Leipzig: Breitkopf & Härtel, 189-.
       (M3 B415) This is not a complete collection of Beethoven's works.

Individual Works or Groups of Works

3. <u>Streichquartette</u> (String Quartets). 17 separate booklets, miniature scores.
       Philharmonia Partituren Nos. 310-326. Wien: Wiener Philharmonischer Ver-
       lag, 192-. (M452 B41mP)

4. <u>String Quartets</u>. 3 vols. miniature scores; 3 vols. separate parts. New
       York: E. F. Kalmus.

5. <u>Quatuors für 2 Violinen, Viola und Violoncell</u>. Separate parts, ed. F. David.
       Leipzig: Peters, 188-. (M451 B41D)

6. <u>Quartette für 2 Violinen, Viola und Violoncell</u>. Separate parts, ed. J.
       Joachim & A. Moser. Leipzig: Peters, 1902-3. (M451 B41J)

7. <u>Quatuors pour 2 violons, alto et violoncelle</u>. Separate parts. Braunschweig:
       Litolff, 19-. (Collection Litolff No. 63) (M451 B41L)

8. <u>Trios für Violine, Bratsche (Viola) und Violoncell</u>. Separate parts. Braun-
       schweig: Litolff, 186-. (M350 B415TL)

9, <u>Trio pour violon, alto et violoncello</u>, Op. 3. Score and parts, ed. H. Böhme.
       Braunschweig: Litolff (No. 1548), 188-. (M314 B415TB)

10. <u>Trio in C minor</u>, Opus 9. Separate parts. New York: International Music Co.,
       1944. (M351 B415T.5I)

11. <u>Serenade in D major</u>, Opus 8, <u>for Violin, Viola & Cello</u>. Separate parts.
       New York: International Music Co., 1948. (M351 B415Sel)

12. <u>Quintet in C major</u>. Opus 29. Separate parts. New York: International
       Music Co., 1944. (M552 B415.2I)

13. <u>Trios für Pianoforte, Violine und Violoncello</u>. 2 vols. Score and separate
       parts, ed. F. David. Leipzig: Peters, 188-. (M312 B41; M312 B41.2)

14. <u>Six Celebrated Trios for Violin, Cello & Piano.</u> Score and separate parts, ed. F. David. New York: International Music Co., 1948. (M312 B41TI)

15. <u>Quintet in E-flat major</u>, Opus 16. For piano, oboe, clarinet, horn, bassoon. Score and separate parts. New York: International Music Co., 1948. (M517 B41SI)

16. <u>Serenade in D major</u>, Opus 25. For flute, violin, viola. Separate parts. New York: International Music Co., 1945. (M362 B41SI)

17. <u>Septet in E-flat major</u>, Opus 20. For violin, viola, horn, clarinet, bassoon, cello, string bass. Separate parts. New York: International Music Co., 1948. (M762 B41sI)

<u>Records</u>

<u>Title</u>	<u>Music</u>	<u>Recording</u>	<u>Call No.</u>

I. String Quartets
   A. Complete sets of the quartets are recorded by the Budapest (Col SL-172, 173, 174), Vegh (HSQ N, O, P), Pascal (CH 1201/12) quartets.

	Title	Music	Recording	Call No.
1.	Op. 18, No. 1 (F)	W, 8	Col 4576 (Budapest) HSQ 43 (Vegh) CH 1201 (Pascal) Vic 1729 (Paganini) West 5203 (Barylli)	
2.	Op. 18, No. 2 (G)	W, 18	Col 4576 (Budapest) HSQ 43 (Vegh) CH 1202 (Pascal) Vic 1729 (Paganini) West 5203 (Barylli)	
3.	Op. 18, No. 3 (D)	W, 26	Col 4577 (Budapest) HSQ 44 (Vegh) CH 1202 (Pascal) West 5211 (Barylli)	
4.	Op. 18, No. 4 (c)	W, 35	Col 4577 (Budapest) HSQ 44 (Vegh) CH 1203 (Pascal) Vic 1052 (Paganini) West 5211 (Barylli)	
5.	Op. 18, No. 5 (A)	W, 43	Col 4578 (Budapest) HSQ 45 (Vegh) CH 1203 (Pascal) Vic 1052 (Paganini) West 5140 (Barylli)	
6.	Op. 18, No. 6 (B-flat)	W, 51	Col 4578 (Budapest) HSQ 45 (Vegh) CH 1204 (Pascal) West 5212 (Barylli)	
7.	Op. 59, No. 1 (F)	W, 59	Col 4155 (Busch) Col 4579 (Budapest) CH 1205 (Pascal) HSQ 41 (Vegh) Lond 673 (New Italian) Vic 7000 (Paganini)	

Ludwig van Beethoven (1770 - 1827)

8. Op. 59, No. 2 (e)   W, 74   Col 4580 (Budapest)
                                          CH 1206 (Pascal)
                                          HSQ 43 (Vegh)
                                          Vic 7001 (Paganini)

9. Op. 59, No. 3 (C)   W, 85   Col 4581 (Budapest)
                                          HSQ 40 (Vegh)
                                          CH 1207 (Pascal)
                                          Vic 1722 (Paganini)

10. Op. 74 (E-flat)   W, 98   Col 4582 (Budapest)
                                          CH 1208 (Pascal)
                                          HSQ 40 (Vegh)
                                          Vic 1722 (Paganini)
                                          CH 42 (Winterthur)

11. Op. 95 (f)   W, 109   Col 4581 (Budapest)
                                          HSQ 40 (Vegh)
                                          CH 1204 (Pascal)
                                          West 5140 (Barylli)

12. Op. 127 (E-flat)   W, 118   Col 4583 (Budapest)
                                          HSQ 46 (Vegh)
                                          CH 1209 (Pascal)

13. Op. 130 (B-flat)   W, 131   Col 4584 (Budapest)
                                          HSQ 47 (Vegh)
                                          West 5129 (Barylli)
                                          CH 1210 (Pascal)

14. Op. 131 (c-sharp)   W, 144   Col 4585 (Budapest)
                                          CH 1211 (Pascal)
                                          HSQ 48 (Vegh)
                                          Vic 1736 (Paganini)
                                          West 5144 (Barylli)

15. Op. 132 (a)   W, 157   Col 4586 (Budapest)
                                          HSQ 49 (Vegh)
                                          CH 1213 (Pascal)
                                          Vic 1179 (Paganini)

16. Op. 135 (F)   W, 177   Col 4587 (Budapest)
                                          HSQ 46 (Vegh)
                                          CH 1212 (Pascal)
                                          Vic 24 (Paganini)
                                          West 5151 (Barylli)

17. Op. 133 (Grosse Fuge)   W, 169   Col 4587 (Budapest)
                                          HSQ 48 (Vegh)
                                          CH 1212 (Pascal)
                                          West 5151 (Barylli)

II. Piano Quartets
18. Op. 152, No. 1 (E-flat)   CH 1215 (Balsam, Pascal)

19. Op. 152, No. 2 (D)

20. Op. 152, No. 3 (G)

III. Quintets
    A. String
        21. Op. 4 (E-flat)   CH 1217 (Gerhard viola,
                                             Pascal)

        22. Op. 29 (C)   CH 1214 (Gerhard, Pascal)

    B. Piano and Winds
        23. Op. 16 (E-flat)   Col 4834 (Serkin)
                                           Vox 9090 (Frugoni)
                                           Strad 616 (Mittman)

IV. Sextets
        24. Op. 71 (E-flat)   West 5003 (Vienna)
             (winds)

        25. Op. 81b (E-flat)   CH 1216 (Speth, Rawyler,
             (two horns and   Pascal)
             strings)

V. Septet
        26. Op. 20 (E-flat)   W, 208   West 5377 (Vienna)
             (violin, viola,   Voc 6470 (Pro Musica)
             cello, bass,
             clarinet, bassoon,
             horn)

VI. Octet
        27. Op. 103 (E-flat)   West 5003 (Vienna)
             (winds)

VII. Serenades
        28. Op. 8 (D) (trio   West 5219
             for strings)   Dec 7506

        29. Op. 25 (D)   W, 306   Dec 9574 (Baker)
             (flute, violin,   Col 2124 (Wummer)
             viola)

VIII. Trios

    A. Piano, Violin, Cello
        30. Op. 1, No. 2 (G)   Col 4573 (Istomin, Schneider,
                                           Casals)

        31. Op. 11 (B-flat)   Col 4571

        32. Op. 70, No. 1 (D) W, 312   Mer 10139 (Albeneri)
             ("Ghost")

        33. Op. 70, No. 2   Mer 10139
             (E-flat)

        34. Op. 97 (B-flat)   W,334   Vic 1020 (Rubinstein, Hei-
             ("Archduke")   fetz, Feuermann)
                                          Mer 10140 (Albeneri)
                                          West 5131 (Badura-Skoda)
                                           Fournier, Janigro)

        35. Op. posth. (B-   Dec 9555 (Mannes, Gimpel,
             flat)   Silva)

B. Strings
    36. Op. 3 (E-flat)   West 5226 (Pougnet,
                                           Riddle, Pini)

    37. Op. 8 (D) (Serenade)   West 5219
                                           Dec 7506 (J. & L. Fuchs,
                                         Rose)

    38. Op. 9, No. 1 (G)   West 5198
                                         Dec 9635 (Bel Arte)

    39. Op. 9, No. 2 (D)   West 5198
                                         Dec 9635

    40. Op. 9, No. 3 (c)   West 5219
                                         Dec 9574 (Fuchs)

FRANZ PETER SCHUBERT (1797 - 1828)

I. **Life.**

1797 Born at Lichtenthal, now part of Vienna, Jan. 31.

1803-07 Taught voice, piano, violin, harmony by his father, a humble school master, and his brothers.

1808-13 Admitted to the school of the Vienna court choir. Trained by Salieri and Eybler. Became leader of the school orchestra. Played viola in chamber music group when at home. Began composing about 1811.

1813-16 Became a teacher in his father's school to avoid military service. Continued to compose.

1817-27 Left home, living with friends when financially destitute. Whole time devoted to composing; wrote symphonies, overtures, piano sonatas, dramatic works, choral music, masses, hundreds of songs. Exploited by publishers, he realized little from his compositions, and only late in life did he receive public recognition.

1828 Died at Vienna, Nov. 19.

II. **Catalogue of Chamber Music.**
   A. String Instruments.
      1. 15 String quartets.
      2. Quartettsatz (1820).
      3. 1 String trio (1817) (violin, viola, cello).
      4. 1 String quintet (1828) (2 violins, 1 viola, 2 cellos).
   B. Piano with other instruments.
      1. 1 Sonata (1817) (violin, piano).
      2. 3 Sonatinas (1816) (violin, piano).
      3. 1 Sonata (1824) (arpeggione or cello, piano).
      4. 2 Trios (piano, violin, cello).
      5. 1 Piano quintet (piano, violin, viola, cello, contra-bass).
      6. 1 Octet (2 violins, viola, cello, bass, clarinet, bassoon, horn).
   C. Miscellaneous.
      1. Nocturne, Op. 148 (1812); Rondo Brilliant, Op. 70 (1826); Phantasie in C, Op. 159 (1827), also known as Sonata No. 4.(all for violin, piano).
      2. Introduction and Variations, Op. 160 (flute, piano).
      3. Sonata movement in B-flat (1812) (piano, violin, cello).
      4. Trio in B-flat (one movement) (violin, viola, cello).
      5. Adagio and Rondo Concertante in F (1816) (piano, violin, viola, cello).
      6. Eine kleine Trauermusik (1813) (2 clarinets, 2 bassoons, contra-bassoon, 2 horns, 2 trombones).
      7. Minuetto and Finale (1813) (2 oboes, 2 clarinets, 2 bassoons, 2 horns)
      8. Quartet (1814) (flute, guitar, viola, cello).
   D. Opus numbers bear no relation to the chronological order of composition, because so few works were published before his death. Quartets Opus 125, Nos. 1 and 2 were composed not later than 1817, Quartet in a, Op. 29, was written in 1824. Quartets are numbered in some editions, in addition to having opus indications, but the numbering is not standard. Quartets are best identified by key.

III. **Chamber Music.**
   A. Schubert wrote a comparatively small amount of chamber music considering his entire output, but it represents a considerable amount of his instrumental music. Some of his immature works, that other composers would

have destroyed, remain. His treatment of the piano in chamber music
formed the foundation for the chamber music with piano of Schumann and
Brahms.

B. Two periods of composition.
    1. Early period includes the first eleven quartets, three sonatinas for
        violin and piano, string trio, and lesser known works.
        a. These works all show Schubert's great melodic gifts and gradual
            development in the skill with which he handled musical ideas and
            the instrumental expression of them.
        b. His early quartets show great deviations in the matter of form.
            They are uneven in quality, and many are overlong. Other weak-
            nesses include too much use of the violins in octaves, much re-
            iteration of the same figure in middle voices, extensive use of
            tremolo, many repeated notes in succession.
    2. Mature period in Schubert's chamber works was reached in 1820 with the
        "Quartettsatz" in c. The Quintet for piano and strings ("The Trout")
        of 1819 belongs between the two periods.
        a. Many of the weaknesses of the early chamber music disappeared. He
            adopted a new way of handling the instruments of the quartet, and
            the form became more concise and the writing more independent.

C. Characteristics of style.
    1. Melody was both his strength and weakness. He used the regular
        division of "song-period" constantly.
    2. Instruments were grouped in twos and played off against each other;
        harmonic groups against each other; a harmonic group against a
        linear phrase.
    3. There was little use of polyphony or polyphonic devices. He preferred
        to invent a new melody, or to modulate freely to other keys rather
        than develop an idea.
    4. Alternating major and minor tonality is characteristic of his style.

IV. String Quartets (Early Period).

A. Six Quartets (1812-13).
    1. Reveal interest in harmonic color and variety. Use of orchestral
        effects: tremolo, unison passages, widely spaced chordal writing.
        Long melodic lines made up of many lyric themes, dramatic climaxes
        and loose forms are characteristic of these quartets.
    2. An early quartet (1814) was written for flute, viola, cello, guitar.
B. Quartet No. 7 in E-flat (c 1814), Op. 125, No. 1.
    1. Allegro moderato C (E-flat); Scherzo, Prestissimo 3/4 (E-flat, Trio,
        c); Adagio 6/8 (E-flat); Allegro 2/4 (E-flat).
    2. First movement has the first themes in the tonic, second theme in the
        dominant, two subsidiary themes.
    3. Scherzo and Adagio are somewhat in early Beethoven style. Brilliant
        Finale.
C. Quartet No. 8 in D (1814).
    1. Allegro 4/4 (D); Andante con moto 4/4 (G-; Menuetto 3/4 (D); Presto
        2/4 (D).
    2. First movement shows development in breadth and power, but the other
        three movements are experimental. All have typical Schubert melodies
        (five in first seventy measures). Uses the characteristic device of
        two themes of equal importance, the second following the first
        immediately.
D. Quartet No. 9 in B-flat (1814), Op. 168.
    1. Allegro ma non troppo 4/4 (B-flat); Andante sostenuto 3/4 (g);
        Menuetto 3/4 (E-flat); Presto 3/4 (B-flat).
    2. Shows a marked advance over the Quartet in D. First movement is in
        clearly defined sections with contrasting melodies, modulations,
        rhythms.

3. Second movement is in lyric style based mostly on the repetition of ideas in various tonalities.
4. Minuet is in Haydn style, with a typical Schubert Trio and much two-part writing in octaves.
5. Presto, in modified sonata-form, is in Scherzo style. Material is based on the first theme; second idea (d) is only a variant of the first theme.

E. Quartet No. 10 in g (1815).
1. Allegro con brio 4/4 (g); Andantino 2/4 (B-flat); Menuetto 3/4 (B-flat); Allegro 2/4 (g).
2. First movement has two contrasting themes in the tonic and dominant. Development of thirty-two measures uses the second theme. Principal subject occurs at the beginning of the Recapitulation in relative major.
3. Second movement has the characteristic hesitation between major and minor, and unusual modulations.
4. Finale is in a modified rondo form.

F. Quartet No. 11 in E (1817), Op. 125, No. 2.
1. Allegro con fuoco 4/4 (E); Andante 2/4 (A); Menuetto 3/4 (E), Rondeau: Allegro vivace 2/4 (E).
2. Less doubling of parts with more four-part writing. New uses of instrumental color.
3. Theme used near the beginning of the first movement becomes, in a varied form, the principal theme of the Finale.
4. Slow movement is exceedingly florid.
5. Finale in rondo form.

V. String Quartets (Mature Period).

A. Quartettsatz in c (1820).
1. Allegro assai 6/8. First movement of an unfinished quartet.
2. Beginning of mature period of chamber music composition. New style of using instruments; each used independently; doubling of parts avoided.

B. Quartet No. 13 in a (1824), Op. 29.
1. Allegro ma non troppo 4/4 (a); Andante 4/4 (C); Menuetto 3/4 (a); Allegro moderato 2/4 (A).
2. This is the only quartet published in Schubert's lifetime. Quiet, somber style and one of his finest works.
3. Principal subject of the slow movement is a melody used in "Rosamunde" ballet music, and the "Impromptu," Op. 142, No. 3.
4. Minuet uses a theme from his setting of Schiller's "Gods of Greece."
5. Finale is in sonata-form. Strong rhythmic and melodic characteristics suggest Hungarian influence.

C. Quartet No. 14 in d (1824), "Death and the Maiden."
1. Allegro 4/4 (d); Andante con moto (theme and variations) C (g); Scherzo: Allegro molto 3/4 (d); Presto 6/8 (d).
2. Outstanding work and the best known of the quartets.
3. First movement has five main ideas, three in the tonic, two in the relative minor. A triplet figure plays an important part in the movement. The second theme (meas. 61) begins the Development (meas. 141). Recapitulation (meas. 198); Coda (meas. 299).
4. Andante is a set of five variations and Coda based on the theme in the accompaniment of the song "Death and the Maiden." Treatment of the theme is less free than with Beethoven; each variation portrays a different mood.
5. Scherzo is vigorous and concise. Form: Scherzo (meas. 1-68) - Trio in D (meas. 69-164) - Scherzo.
6. Finale is a long, powerful movement in rondo form: A (meas. 1-88)-

B (meas. 89-317) - A with short Development (meas. 318-446 - B (meas. 447-651) - A and Coda (meas.652-754). "Erlkönig" theme is introduced (meas. 134).
  D. Quartet No. 15 in G (1826), Op. 161.
    1. Allegro molto moderato 3/4 (G); Andante un poco molto 4/4 (e); Scherzo: Allegro vivace 3/4 (b); Allegro assai 6/8 (G).
    2. Schubert's last quartet. It uses many orchestral effects, with emphasis on shifting harmonies, rather than melodic lines. Characteristic alternation of major and minor found in the first and last movements.

VI. Two Quintets.

  A. Quintet, "The Trout" in A (1819), Op. 114.
    1. Allegro vivace 4/4 (A); Andante 3/4 (F); Scherzo: Presto 3/4 (A); Andantino: Theme and Variations 2/4 (D); Finale: Allegro giusto 2/4 (A).
    2. Instrumentation: piano, violin, viola, cello, contra-bass. First work in which Schubert used one of his songs as the subject for variations. (Quartet No. 14 is dated 1824). The work is unusual in the use of the string bass. First composition by any major composer for piano and four strings, but not strictly speaking a piano quintet as the usual string quartet combination is not used. Quintets by Mozart and Beethoven are for piano and wind instruments.
    3. First movement is in sonata-form; second theme (meas. 54) is given to cello. Development begins in measure 147; Recapitulation in measure 210.
    4. Second movement is in three contrasting sections, F, f-sharp, D, ending in G, which are repeated a minor third higher in A-flat, a, F.
    5. Third movement is a Scherzo (meas. 1-104) and Trio (meas. 105-170).
    6. Fourth movement is a theme and six variations on "The Trout." The sixth variation has the piano accompaniment from the song.
    7. Fifth movement is an Allegro giusto in A which has a Hungarian rhythm. Sonata-form without a Development section and with a Recapitulation (meas. 237) which is an exact transposition of the Exposition up a fifth. Second theme in the Exposition begins in measure 84.
  B. Quintet in C (1828), Op. 163.
    1. Allegro ma non troppo 4/4 (C); Adagio 12/8 (E); Scherzo: Presto 3/4 (C); Allegretto C (C).
    2. Instrumentation: 2 violins, viola, 2 cellos. Generally considered Schubert's finest chamber work. The use of a second cello gives the first cello greater melodic freedom.
    3. Allegro uses two lyric themes and subsidiary melodies. Great variety in the use of the instruments.
    4. Adagio is in three contrasting sections in E, f, E.
    5. Scherzo (3/4) is in strongly contrasting moods and meters. Trio (4/4) is an Andante sostenuto in D-flat.
    6. Finale begins in c, but is in C from measure 19. The tempo increases at the end to Più allegro, concluding with a Più presto.

VII. Two Piano Trios.

  A. Trio in B-flat (1827), Op. 99 (piano, violin, cello).
    1. Allegro moderato 4/4 (B-flat); Andante un poco mosso 6/8 (E-flat); Scherzo 3/4 (B-flat); Rondo 2/4 (B-flat).
    2. Written for a trio composed of Schuppanzigh and Linke (friends of Beethoven and members of the Rasoumowsky Quartet) and the pianist von Bocklet. The two trios represent Schubert at his best.
    3. First movement is in Sonata-form. It is built on two contrasting themes and fragments, which are repeated with different harmonic

effects.
4. Second movement is in three sections.
5. Finale is a movement of great length in rondo form. It is based on a folk-like melody.

B. Trio in E-flat (1827), Op. 100 (piano, violin, cello).
1. Allegro 3/4 (E-flat); Andante con moto 2/4 (c); Scherzo: Allegro moderato 3/4 (E-flat); Allegro moderato 6/8 (E-flat).
2. First movement has many changes of tonality and signature. The characteristic accompaniment figure of the first movement reappears in the last movement, an unusual device for Schubert.
3. Second movement is in the form of a March.
4. Third movement is based on a canon between the piano and strings in octaves. The second part of the movement is based on a modified inversion of the canon theme.
5. Finale is the longest of the four long movements. It is in the typical Schubert sonata-form. The principal subject of the slow movement (meas. 275, 693), is introduced, but in the tempo and rhythm of the Finale. Second theme (meas. 73) is modified (meas. 125) and developed (meas. 163). Development (meas. 315); Recapitulation (meas. 441), second theme is in f (meas. 559).

BIBLIOGRAPHY
Books

1. Abraham, G. E.   The Music of Schubert, ed. by G. Abraham. New York: W. W. Norton, 1947. (ML410 S38A15)

2. Antcliffe, H.   Schubert. London: G. Bell and Sons, 1910. (ML410 S38A62)

3. Bie, O.   Schubert, the Man. New York: Dodd, Mead & Co., 1928. (ML410 S38B58U)

4. Brent-Smith, A.   Schubert - Quartet in D minor and Octet. New York: Oxford University Press, 1927. (MT145 S38S64)

5. Deutsch, O. E.   Franz Schubert's Letters and Other Writings. Transl. by V. Savile. New York: A. A. Knopf, 1928. (ML410 S38D48DS)

6. Deutsch, O. E.   Schubert, A Documentary Biography. Transl. by Eric Blom. London: J. M. Dent, 1947. (ML410 S38D48B)

7. Deutsch, O. E.   Schubert. Thematic Catalogue of all his Works in Chronological Order. London: Dent, 1951. (ML134 S38D48T)

8. Duncan, E.   Schubert. New York: E. P. Dutton & Co., 1934. (ML410 S38D91.2)

9. Einstein, A.   Schubert; A Musical Portrait. New York: Oxford University Press, 1951. (ML410 S38E35)

10. Flower, W. N.   Franz Schubert, the Man and His Circle. London: Cassell, 1928. (ML410 S38F64)

11. Humiston, W. H.   Schubert. New York: Breitkopf Publications, 1925. (ML385 L77)

12. Kobald, K.   Franz Schubert and His Times. Transl. by B. Marshall. New York: A. A. Knopf, 1928. (ML410 S38K75M)

13. Mason, D. G.   The Romantic Composers. New York: Macmillan, 1926.
    (ML390 M39r)

14. Schauffler, R.H. Franz Schubert: the Ariel of Music. New York: G. P. O
    Putnam, 1949. (ML410 S38S31)

15. Wells-Harrison, W. Schubert's Compositions for Piano and Strings. New York:
    Scribner, 1915. (MT145 S38w)

16. Whitaker-Wildon, C. Franz Schubert, Man and Composer. London: W. Reeves,
    1928. (ML410 S38W577)

Periodicals

1. Adler, G.   "Schubert and the Viennese Classic School," MQ 14 (1928),
    473.

2. Bailly, L.   "Schubert's Chamber Music," MusCo (1928), 7.

3. Boughton, R.   "Schubert and Melodic Design," MT 69 (1928), 881.

4. Brown, M.   "Small Latin and Less Counterpoint," MR 8 (1947), 175.

5. Brown, M.   "Schubert and Neapolitan Relationships," MT 85 (1944), 43.

6. Capell, R.   "Schubert's Style," MT 69 (1928), 304.

7. Dale, K.   "Schubert's Indebtedness to Haydn," ML 21 (1940), 23.

8. Dent, E.   "The Style of Schubert," Dominant Vol. 1, No. 8, June 1928.

9. Deutsch, O. E.   "The Chronology of Schubert's String Quartets, ML 24
    (1943), 25.

10. Engel, C.   "Schubert's Fame," MQ 14 (1928), 457.

11. Jean-Aubrey, G.   "The Spirit of Schubert," Chesterian 10.

12. Költzsch, H.   "Schubert and the Romantic Problem," ML 20 (1939), 130.

13. Laciar, S.   "The Chamber Music of Franz Schubert," MQ 14 (1928), 515.

14. Smith, A. B.   "Franz Schubert," New Mus Rev 30 (1931), 425.

15. Schubert, F.   "Franz Schubert," special issue, MusCo (April 12, 1928).

Music

1. Wier, A.   Chamber Music of Haydn and Schubert. New York: Longmans,
    Green and Co., 1940.

2. Werke (Complete works of Schubert). Leipzig: Breitkopf und Härtel.
    (M3 S384). Chamber music in volumes as follows:
        Series 3   Octet
               4-6   Quintet, Quartets, Trio for strings
               7   Part I, Piano Quintet and Quartet
               7   Part II, Piano Trios
               8   Piano and one ihstrument
               21   No. 1-31 Instrumental Music

3. Eulenberg, E., ed. Kleine Partiturausgabe. (Miniature scores) (M451 or 452
    S384mP) (Payne, A.) Leipzig: Eulenberg, 189-.
    a. No. 11   Quartet in d, Op. posth.
    b. No. 39   Quartet in G, Op. 161.
    c. No. 40   Quartet in a, Op. 29.
    d. No. 60   Octet in F, Op. 166.
    e. No. 84   Piano Trio in B-flat, Op. 99.
    f. No. 85   Piano Trio in E-flat, Op. 100.
    g. No. 116   Quartet in B-flat, Op. 168.
    h. No. 117   Quartet in g, Op. posth.
    i. No. 118   Piano Quintet in A, Op. 114.
    j. No. 119   Quartet in E, Op. 125, No. 2.
    k. No. 120   Quartet in E-flat, Op. 125, No. 1.
    l. No. 121   Quartets in D and e, Op. posth.
    m. No. 233   Nocturne (Piano Trio) in E-flat, Op. 148.

4. Philharmonia, ed. Taschenpartituren.(Ministure scores). Wien: Philharmon-
    ischer Verlag, 192-. (M451 or 452 S384mPh).
    a. No. 351   Quartet in am Op. 29.
    b. No. 352   Quartet in d, Op. posth.
    c. No. 353   Quartet in G, Op. 161.
    d. No. 354   String Quintet in C, Op. 163.
    e. No. 355   Quartet in B-flat, Op. 168.
    f. No. 356   Octet in F, Op. 166.
    g. No. 369   String Trio in B-flat.
    h. No. 375   Piano Quintet in A, Op. 114.

Individual Works

5. Quatuors pour 2 violons, alto et violoncello par Schubert. Separate parts.
    Braunshweig et New York: H. Litolff, 186-. (Publ. nos. 2812-2815)
    (M451 S384L)

6. Quartette für 2 Violinen, Viola & Violoncell. 2 vols. ed. F. David. Sep-
    arate parts. Leipzig: Peters, 186-. (M451 S384D)

7. Trout-Quintet, Op. 114. Score and separate parts. New York: International
    Music Co., 1943. (M512 S384I)

8. Quintet in C major, Op. 163. Separate parts. New York: International
    Music Co., 1943. (M552 S384I)

9. Trio No. 2, in B-flat major. For violin, viola, cello. Separate parts.
    New York: International Music Co., 1947. (M351 S384.2I)

10. Trios für Pianoforte, Violine und Violoncell, ed. F. David. Score and
    separate parts. Leipzig: Peters, 188-. (M312 S384t)

11. Octet in F major, Op. 166. Separate parts. New York: International Music
    Co., 1948. (M862 S384I)

12. Quartett für Flöte, Gitarre, Bratsche und Violoncell. Score & separate
    parts. München: Drei Masken Verlag, 1926. (M482 S384)

Records

Title	Music	Recording	Call No.

I. String Quartets.
    A. The first twelve quartets are recorded by Westminster and played by the

Vienna Konzerthaus Quartet.

1. No. 1 (B-flat), No. 2
   (C); No. 3 (B-flat)   West 5204

2. No. 4 (C); No. 5 (E-
   flat)   West 5210

3. No. 6 (D)   West 5224

4. No. 7 (D); No. 8 (B-
   flat) (Op. 168)   West 5110

5. No. 9 (g)   West 5224

6. No. 10 (E-flat); No.11   W, 310   West 5222
   (E) (Op. 125, No. 1)

7. No. 12 "Quartettsatz" (c)   West 5210
   (Op posth)   Dec 4040 (Koeckert)

8. No. 13, Op. 29 (a)   W, 270   Col 194 (Budapest)
                                                    Lond 587 (Vegh)
                                                    Lond 668 (New Italian)

9. No. 14, Op. posth. (d)   W, 295   Col 194 (Budapest)
   ("Death and the Maiden")   Vox 8810 (Barchet)
                                                    Vic 1058 (Amadeus)
                                                    West 5052 (Vienna)

10. No. 15, Op. 161 (G)   W, 280   Col 194 (Budapest)
                                                    West 5041 (Vienna)
                                                    Mer 10104 (Fine Arts)

II. Miscellaneous
11. Quartet for Flute, Gui-   Per 518
    tar, Viola, Cello

12. Quintet for Strings,   W, 192   Col 4437 (Budapest)
    Op. 163 (C)   Col 4714 (Prades)
                                                    West 5033 (Vienna)

13. Quintet for Piano and   W, 212   Dec 9707 (Aeschbacher, Koe-
    Strings, Op. 114 (A)   ckert)
    ("The Trout")   MGM 3128 (Pressler, Guilet)
                                                    West 5025 (Badura-Skoda,
                                                        Vienna)
                                                    Col 4317 (Horszowski, Budapest)
                                                    Vic M-312 (Schnabel, Pro-Arte)
                                                        (78 RPM)

14. Octet in F, Op. 166   W, 161   Lond 1049 (Vienna)
    (string quartet, bass,   West 5094 (Vienna Konzerthaus)
    clarinet, horn, bassoon)   Vox 6970 (Vienna Symphony)

III. Trios
   A. Violin, Cello, Piano
15. No. 1, Op. 99 (B-flat)   W, 235   Mer 10106 (Albeneri)
                                                    Vic 1017 (Heifetz, Feuermann,
                                                        Rubinstein)

                                        Vic 1141 (Thibaud, Cortot,
                                          Casals)
                                        West 5188 (Fournier, Janigro,
                                          Badura-skoda)
                                        Col 4715 (Schneider, Casals,
                                          Istomin)

16. No. 2, Op. 100 (E-flat) W, 251   Col 4654 (A. Busch, H. Busch,
                                          Serkin)
                                        West 5121 (Fournier, Janigro,
                                          Badura-Skoda)
                                        Mer 10107 (Albeneri)
                                        Col 4716 (Schneider, Casals,
                                          Horowitz)

     B. Violin, Viola, Cello
17. Trio in B-flat   West 5223 (Vienna)

OUTLINE VI

JACOB LUDWIG FELIX MENDELSSOHN (1809 - 1847)

I. Life.

1809   Born at Hamburg, Feb. 4, into a wealthy and cultured family. Moved to Berlin (1812). Name Bartholdy was added to Mendelssohn when the family became Protestants.

1816   Studied with Berger, Zelter, Henning, Mme. Bigot (in Paris), and Moscheles (1824). Met famous artists, writers, and other distinguished people at his home.

1820   Began to compose at the age of eleven. By 1825 he was an accomplished pianist, organist, violinist and composer. His Overture to "A Midsummer Night's Dream" was written in 1825 at the age of sixteen.

1829   Directed the Singakademie in a performance of Bach's "St. Matthew Passion" (1829), the first since Bach's death. Traveled in England, Italy, Switzerland, France. Declined the offer of position in Berlin University.

1833   Became music director at Düsseldorf (1833-35); conductor of Gewandhaus Orchestra in Leipzig (1835). Made many trips, especially to England. Friendship with Schumann.

1837   Married Cécile Jeanrenaud, daughter of a Swiss clergyman. Received an honorary Ph. D. degree from the University of Leipzig.

1843   Organized the Conservatory of Leipzig, which had a distinguished faculty, including Schumann. Music director at courts at Berlin and Dresden; continued conducting and traveling.

1847   Died in Leipzig, Nov. 4, at the age of thirty-eight.

II. Catalogue of Chamber Music.

A. Six String Quartets and Quartet movements.
1. E-flat, Op. 12; a, Op. 13; D, e, E-flat, Op. 44; f, Op. 80.
2. Quartet movements Op. 81, Andante Scherzo, Capriccio, Fugue.
B. Two String Quintets (2 violins, 2 violas, cello).
1. Op. 18 in A; Op. 87 in B-flat.
C. String Octet in E-flat, Op. 20 (4 violins, 2 violas, 2 cellos).
D. Three Sonatas with Piano.
1. Sonata for Violin and Piano, Op. 14 in f.
2. 2 sonatas for Cello and Piano
   a. Op. 45 in B-flat; Op. 58 in D.
E. Trios with Piano.
1. Op. 49 in d; Op. 66 in c (piano, violin, cello).
2. 2 Pieces Op. 113 in F; Op. 114 in d (piano, clarinet, basset-horn).
F. Three Piano Quartets.
1. Op. 1 in c; Op. 2 in f; Op. 3 in b.
G. Sextet, Op. 110 in D (piano, violin, 2 violas, cello, contra-bass).

III. Chamber Music.

A. First chamber music (Piano Quartets Op. 1, 2, 3) was written before the age of fifteen.
1. Mendelssohn's style was based on a natural sense of form and good taste. His music is correct, suave, polished, and his melodies are

facile and charming, but rarely intense.
   2. He was especially successful in Scherzo movements and developed a new
      type in duple meter, in large rondo form. The old minuet-scherzo with
      trio disappeared.
   3. A conservative Romanticist as regards form, he generally followed
      existing paths.

IV. String Quartets.

   A. Op. 13 (a) (1827).
      1. Unusual in the use of his song "Is it true" (Op. 9, No. 1) at begin-
         ning and end. Second theme of the first movement is used in the
         Finale (cyclic). Recitative is used in the slow movement.
   B. Op. 12 (E-flat) (1829).
      1. Shows characteristics of his mature style, although written at the age
         of twenty. Introduction suggests Beethoven's Op. 74 ("Harp" quartet).
         Second theme is related rhythmically to the first. The mood is lyric
         throughout.
      2. "Canzonetta" takes the place of a Scherzo. Makes effective use of
         pizzicato and staccato, with a humorous conclusion.
      3. Finale uses themes from the first movement (cyclic).
   C. Three String Quartets, Op. 44 (1837-38).
      1. Op. 44, No. 1 (D).
         a. Brilliant first and last movements in orchestral style. A melod-
            ious Minuet and an Andantino in "song-without-words" style com-
            plete the work.
      2. Op. 44, No. 2 (e).
         a. Remarkable elfin-like Scherzo. Finale in rondo form, with the
            principal theme in country-dance style.
      3. Op. 44, No. 3 (E-flat).
         a. An outstanding quartet. It includes fugal sections, imitations,
            clear forms, striking themes, melodious melodies, a sparkling
            Scherzo.
   D. Op. 80 (f) (1847).
      1. Written nine years after Op. 44, possibly inspired by the death of his
         sister. A solemn work, definitely inferior to other quartets.
   E. Quartet movements, Op. 81.
      1. Andante (E) (1847); Scherzo (a) (1847); Capriccio (e) (1843); Fugue
         (E-flat) (1847). Published in 1850 as Op. 81.

V. Two String Quintets (2 violins, 2 violas, cello).

   A. Op. 18 (A) (1826, rewritten 1832).
      1. Not a distinguished work, although the Scherzo with its fugato treat-
         ment of the main theme is typical Mendelssohn.
   B. Op. 87 (B-flat) (1845).
      1. The only outstanding movement is the Adagio. There is much use of
         orchestral tremolos, and the themes are generally undistinguished.

VI. String Octet, Op. 20 (E-flat) (1825) (4 violins, 2 violas, 2 cellos).

   A. This is the first string octet which treats the two quartets as an eight-
      voiced work (in Spohr's octets, the second quartet plays an accompanying
      or antiphonal part). All instruments take part in the ensemble, although
      the brilliant first violin sometimes dominates. Many orchestral effects.
      Mendelssohn said that the work should be played in symphonic style.
   B. First movement opens with vigorous theme (1st violin) accompanied by
      tremolo and syncopations. A fanfare motive enters in measure 21 and a
      quiet second theme in measure 68. Recapitulation varies the material
      somewhat; Coda begins with a fanfare motive.

    C. Scherzo is staccato and soft throughout; the outstanding movement of the
Octet. Later arranged for orchestra by Mendelssohn.

    D. Finale begins with fugal exposition and the Scherzo movement reappears.

VII. Two Trios for Piano, Violin, Cello.

    A. Op. 49 in d (1839).

        1. Trios are among his best chamber works. Perfection of form and de-
tail is everywhere in evidence. Schumann considered Op. 49 comparable
to Beethoven's B-flat and D trios and Schubert's in E-flat.

        2. Scherzo, as usual, and the Andante con Moto are outstanding movements.

    B. Op. 66 in c (1845).

        1. Allegro energico begins with a strong theme emphasizing the key of c,
followed by a contrasting expressive second theme. One of his finest
movements.

        2. Melodious Andante expressivo is followed by a virtuoso Scherzo.

        3. Finale is another masterpiece. Agitated principal theme begins with
the interval of the ninth. The contrasting second theme is not much
used. Coda in C uses the first theme.

VIII. Sextet, Op. 110 in D (1824) (piano, violin, 2 violas, cello, contra-bass).

    A. An experimental early work of little merit. It shows, however, Mendels-
sohn's gift for clear form. The Minuet, in unusual 6/8 time, appears in
the Finale before the Coda.

BIBLIOGRAPHY
Books

1. Benedict, Sir J.   Sketch of the Life and Works of the late Felix Mendelssohn-Bartholdy. London: GF. Murray, 1850. (ML410 M53B46)

2. Kaufman, S.   Mendelssohn, a Second Elijah. New York: T. Y. Crowell
Co., 1934. (ML410 M53K2)

3. Lampadius, W.A.   The Life of Felix Mendelssohn-Bartholdy. Transl. by W. L.
Gage. New York: H. Ditson and Co., 1887. (ML410 M53L23.3)

4. Mason, D. G.   The Romantic Composers. New York: Macmillan, 1926.
(ML390 M39r)

5. Mendelssohn-Bartholdy, F. Thematisches Verzeichnis der im Druck erschienenen
Compositionen von Felix Mendelssohn-Bartholdy. Leipzig: Breitkopf &
Härtel, 187-. (ML134 M53.2)

6. Nohl, L.   Letters of Distinguished Musicians: Gluck, Haydn, P. E.
Bach, Weber, Mendelssohn. Transl. by Lady Wallace. London: Longmans,
Green & Co., 1867. (ML90 N779W)

7. Rockstro, W. S.   Mendelssohn. London: S. Low, Marston & Co., 190-.
(ML410 M53R68).

8. Selden-Goth, G.   Letters of Felix Mendelssohn-Bartholdy. New York: Pan-
theon, 1945. (ML410 M53S46)

9. Stratton, S. S.   Mendelssohn. New York: E. P. Dutton, 1934.
(ML410 M53S91.2)

Periodicals

1. Foss, H. J.   "A Commentary upon Mendelssohn," _MT_ (1924), 404.

2. Riker, C.   "Review of Mendelssohn's Letters," _Kenyon Review_ 7 (1945), 728.

3. Scott, C.   "The Mendelssohnian Sympathy," _The Sackbut_ (Jan. 1925), 165.

4. Smith, A. B.   "The Workmanship of Mendelssohn," _ML_ (1923), 18.

5. Watson, S. R.   "Mendelssohn: The first Maestro," _MusAm_ (1947), 5.

6. Whittaker, W. G.   "Mendelssohn's Octet," _MT_ (1933), 322.

Music

1. Wier, A. E.   _Miscellaneous Chamber Works._ New York: Longmans, Green & Co., 1940.

2. Mendelssohn-Bartholdy, F. _Werke._ (Complete Edition). 19 vols. in 37. Leipzig: Breitkopf & Härtel, 1874-77. (M3 M537)

3. _Mendelssohn's Chamber Music._ Miniature scores. Leipzig: Eulenburg, 188-. The following are bound together in 2 vols.: (M178 M53m)
Vol. I: Quartets, Op. 12, 13, 44 (Nos. 1-3), 80, 81.
Vol. II: Quintets, Op. 18, 87; Octet, Op. 20; Trios Op. 49, 66.

4. _Octet for Strings_, Op. 20. Score. New York: International Music Co., 1949. (M852 M537Im)

5. _Octet for Strings_, Op. 20. Separate parts. New York: International Music Co., 1948. (M852 M537I)

6. _Quartette für Pianoforte, Violine, Bratsche (Viola), Violoncell._ Op. 1, 2, 3. Rev. by F. Hermann. Score and separate parts. Leipzig: Peters, 190- (M411 M53)

7. _Quartets_, Op. 12 and Op. 44, Nos. 1, 2, 3. Separate parts. New York: International Music Co., 1947. (M451 M537I)

8. _Quartette für 2 Violinen, Bratsche (Viola) und Violoncello._ Separate parts. Peters, 189-. (M451 M537P.2)

9. _Quintette für 2 Violinen, 2 Bratsche (Violas), Violoncell_, Op. 18 und 67. Leipzig: Peters, 189-. (M551 M53)

Records

Title	Music	Recording	Call No.
I. String Quartets			
1. No. 1, Op. 12 (E-flat)	W, 215	West 5220 (Curtis) Mer 10065 (Fine Arts)	
2. No. 2, Op. 12 (a)		Col 4921 (New Music)	
3. No. 3, Op. 44, No. 1 (D)	W, 222	West 5220 (Curtis)	

4. No. 4, Op. 44, No. 2   Str 615 (Endres)
    (e)

5. No. 5, Op. 44, No. 3   Col 4921 (New Music)
    (E-flat)   Str 615 (Endres)

II. String Quintets
    6. No. 1, Op. 18 (A)   CH 1172 (Gerhard, Pascal)

    7. No. 2, Op. 87 (B-flat)   CH 1172 (Gerhard, Pascal)

III. Miscellaneous
    8. Quartet, Op. 2 (f)   CH 1095 (Balsam, Guilet,
        (piano and strings)   Brieff, Laporte)

    9. Sextet, Op. 110 (F)   MGM 3107 (Pressler, Gordon,
        (piano, violin, 2 violas,   Sklar, Guilet)
        cello, bass)

    10. Octet, Op. 20 (E-flat)   Lond 859 (Vienna)
         (two string quartets)

    11. Two Concert Pieces, Op.   West 5024 (Bartosek, Wlach,
         113, 114 (bassett horn,   Demus)
         clarinet, piano)

    12. Trio No. 1, Op. 49   W, 195 Vic 1119 (Rubinstein, Heifetz,
         (d) (piano, violin,   Piatigorsky)
         cello)   Vox 9160 (Bolzano)

    13. Trio No. 2, Op. 66   Vox 9160 (Bolzano)
         (c) (piano, violin,
         cello)

OUTLINE VII
ROBERT ALEXANDER SCHUMANN (1810 - 1856)

I. Life.

1810   Born at Zwickau, Saxony, June 8. Father was a book seller and publisher.

1825   Became attracted by fantastic, sentimental, romantic writings of Jean Paul (Richter).

1828   Sent to University of Leipzig to study law and in 1829 to Heidelberg. Continued the study of piano.

1830   Left University to study piano with Frederick Wieck; injured hand with a mechanical device and turned to composition. Wrote only piano music up to 1839.

1834   Founded the Neue Zeitschrift für Musik, which he edited until 1844. This journal exerted a wide influence on musical life and taste of the time. Began his friendship with Mendelssohn.

1838   Visited Vienna and recovered many Schubert manuscripts.

1840   Married Clara Wieck. Composed many songs, orchestral compositions (1841), chamber music (1843). Often went on tours with his wife, an excellent pianist.

1843   Became a member of the faculty of the new Leipzig Conservatory. Ill health prompted a move to Dresden (1844).

1850   Followed Hiller as musical director at Düsseldorf, but was not a success as a conductor. Continued composing.

1853   Forced to retire because of a mental breakdown. Meeting with Brahms.

1854   Attempted to take his own life by drowning in the Rhine. He spent his remaining days in a sanatorium in a state of mental derangement.

1856   Died July 29 near Bonn.

II. Catalogue of Chamber Music.

A. Three String Quartets , Op. 41: No. 1 (a); No. 2 (F); No. 3 (A) (1842).
B. Piano Quintet in E-flat, Op. 44 (1842).
C. Piano Quartet in E-flat, Op. 47 (1842).
D. Trios for Piano, Violin, Cello.
   1. Trio in d, Op. 63 (1847).
   2. Trio in F, Op. 80 (1847).
   3. Trio in g, Op. 110 (1851).
   4. Fantasiestücke, Op. 88 (1842).
E. Sonatas for Piano, Violin.
   1. Sonata in a, Op. 105 (1851).
   2. Sonata in d, Op. 121 (1851).
F. Miscellaneous.
   1. Märchenbilder Suite (piano, viola), Op. 113 (1851).
   2. Fantasiestücke (piano, clarinet), Op. 73 (1849).
   3. Märchenerzählungen (piano, clarinet), Op. 132 (1853).
   4. Adagio and Allegro (piano, horn), Op. 70 (1849).

5. 3 Romances (piano, oboe), Op. 94 (1849).
6. 5 Stücke im Volkston (piano, cello), Op. 104 (1849).

III. Chamber Music.

A. Schumann's first and greatest chamber music was composed in 1842. He
    studied the string quartets of Haydn and Mozart and sought advice of
    Mendelssohn, Joachim, David. Generally most successful in small forms
    and mood pieces.
B. Characteristics of his style are: sudden changes of mood; a tendency to
    write in pianistic style for string instruments; use of minor keys (es-
    pecially a, d); dotted rhythms; rising and falling scale lines; falling
    minor third returning a half step upward; falling fifths; lyric unity;
    melodic doubling; basic sonority of open octave; standard key relation-
    ships; sudden dynamic contrasts; rhythmic accents on weak beats.
C. Romantic characteristics appear frequently in the quiet, expressive
    melodies. Schumann was frequently unable, in his chamber music, to sus-
    tain a high level of inspiration. He was unable to give up classicism
    entirely, or to give himself up completely to romanticism.

IV. String Quartets, Op. 41. Dedicated to Mendelssohn.

A. Op. 41, No. 1 (a), (1842).
    1. Introduzione, Andante expressivo (a) - Allegro (F).
        a. Introduction is based on imitation and modulates to F for the
            Allegro. Principal theme contains material for the whole movement.
        b. First section (meas. 34-75) is based on a theme in two parts.
            Second begins in measure 56 with characteristic accents in the
            second half of the measure. A new theme (meas. 76) is treated in
            a short fugato followed by a second fugato, which is an extension
            of the second part of the first theme (meas. 99-136).
        c. The Development (meas. 151-252) uses material already presented,
            with great freedom and interesting modulations. Recapitulation
            (meas. 253-355) is followed by a Coda (meas. 365-374).
    2. Scherzo (a).
        a. Three sections: Scherzo in 6/8 (meas. 1-82); Intermezzo in Alla
            Breve (meas. 83-115); Recapitulation of Scherzo (meas. 27. Use of
            a germ rhythm recalls Beethoven. Intermezzo in place of a Trio
            shows effort to change classic forms. Scherzo is often the second
            movement.
    3. Adagio (F).
        a. Three-part form with use of the variation principle: Introduction
            (meas. 1-3); Part I (meas. 4-28); Part II, free variation of Part
            I (meas. 29-43); Part III, varied recapitulation of Part I (meas.
            44-62); Coda uses Introductory figures (meas. 63-67).
        b. Part I includes: first theme (meas. 4), second theme (meas. 16),
            varied recapitulation of first theme (meas. 20-27), modulation to
            A-flat for Part II (meas. 28). Sudden contrast of mood in the
            middle section is a characteristic of Schumann's style.
    4. Presto (a - A).
        a. Sonata-form: Exposition (meas. 1-80); Development (meas. 81-209);
            expanded Recapitulation (meas. 210-289); Coda (meas. 290-324). Key
            of F appears in the Development, returning to a for the Recapitula-
            tion and to A for the Coda.
        b. Basic material of the movement consists of ascending broken thirds
            derived from the first theme. Subsidiary theme (meas. 43) intro-
            duces a contrasting descending scale line. Another subsidiary
            theme enters (meas. 63) which is used in the Development with the
            first interval inverted. "Musette" in A (meas. 258) is followed
            by the Coda (meas. 290), which uses broken third and descending

scale themes.   The first theme does not appear.
B. Op. 41, No. 2 (F).
    1. Allegro Vivace (F).
        a. Sonata-form with material derived from the first theme. Exposition
            (meas. 1-96); Development (meas. 97-181); Recapitulation (meas.
            182-261); Coda (meas. 261-281). Secondary theme (meas. 68) and
            closing theme (meas. 80) are an extension of the smooth-flowing,
            romantic principal theme.
    2. Andante, quasi Variazioni (A-flat).
        a. Variations in rhapsodic style in three parts.
            1) Part I: Principal theme (meas. 1-8) followed by a secondary sub-
                ject (meas. 8-16), possibly a variation of the principal theme,
                and an altered version (meas. 16-32) of the principal section.
            2) Part II: First variation (meas. 32-48); second (meas. 48-64);
                third (meas. 64-76); fourth (meas. 76-89).
            3) Part III (meas. 89-105) is a shortened recapitulation of Part I.
                Coda (meas. 105-112).
    3. Scherzo: Presto (c).
        a. Scherzo (meas. 1-88); Trio (meas. 89-122); Scherzo (meas. 122-170);
            Coda (meas. 171-195).
        b. A brilliant, difficult movement with a Trio in the style of Mendels-
            sohn.
    4. Allegro molto vivace (F).
        a. Sonata-form: Exposition (meas. 1-50); Development (meas. 51-152);
            Recapitulation (meas. 153-195); Coda (meas. 195-227).
        b. There is a strong resemblance to the finale of his "Spring Sym-
            phony," Op. 38 (1841) in principal themes and ascending scales
            (meas. 28-35). The movement makes much use of jagged imitations.
C. Op. 41, No. 3 (A) (1842).
    1. Andante expressivo-Allegro molto moderato (A).
        a. Sonata-form: Introduction (meas. 1-7); Exposition (meas. 8-101);
            Development (meas. 102-145); shortened Recapitulation (meas. 146-
            209); Coda (meas. 210-226).
        b. Falling interval of a perfect fifth is used in various ways. Off-
            beat accompaniment passages suggest pianistic style.
    2. Assai agitato (f).
        a. Variations with the theme appearing after the third variation.
            Variation I (meas. 1-45); Variation II (meas. 49-96); Variation III,
            L'istesso tempo (meas. 97-144); Theme, un poco Adagio (meas. 145-
            192); Variation IV (meas. 192-224); Coda (meas. 224-255).
        b. There is variety of mood, with the usual variation types avoided.
            Type of variation is that used by Sibelius.
    3. Adagio molto (D).
        a. Three-part form: Part I (meas. 1-44); Part II (meas. 44-77); Part
            III (meas. 77-105); Coda (meas. 94-105).
        b. First theme appears in measures 1, 44, 77; second theme in measures
            19, 58, 94 (suggested).
    4. Allegro molto vivace (A).
        a. Rondo combined with large ternary form.
            1) Part I: main theme (meas. 1); first subordinate theme (meas. 14);
                main theme (meas. 34); second subordinate theme (meas. 48); main
                theme (meas. 64); third subordinate theme (meas. 72).
            2) Part II: main theme (meas. 112); first subordinate theme (meas.
                126); main theme (meas. 146); second subordinate theme (meas.
                160); main theme (meas. 176); third subordinate theme (meas. 184).
            3) Part III: main theme, Coda (meas. 224).
        b. Main theme is in dotted-note rhythm (used in third movement) and
            appears seven times. There are three subordinate themes, each ap-
            pearing twice.

V.   Piano and Strings.
   A. Quintet for Piano and Strings in E-flat, Op. 44 (1843).
      1. First piano quintet with piano and string quartet. Second Trio of
          the second movement was revised at Mendelssohn's suggestion. Piano
          balances the four strings; often introduces themes; plays almost
          continuously (only six measures rest in the entire work); accompani-
          ment figures often broken chords; arpeggiated chords are rare; much
          use of full chords, often five-part with any note doubled; piano
          often doubles strings for greater sonority.
      2. Allegro brilliante (E-flat).
          a. Sonata-form: first theme passes through several keys; second theme
              is introduced by the piano (meas. 51) and stated by cello (meas.
              57); codetta (meas. 108) uses part of the first theme in the
              dominant.
          b. Development begins with the establishment of the key of a-flat;
              first theme is then introduced (meas. 1-28); piano treats measures
              3 and 4 of the first theme in diminution; modulations from a-flat
              through e-flat, b-flat, f, c. The first theme is in f (meas. 168)
              followed by modulations through g-flat, d-flat, a-flat, e-flat and
              finally through a chromatic line to the dominant of E-flat.
          c. Recapitulation (meas. 207) repeats material of the Exposition al-
              most exactly with the second theme in the tonic.
      3. In modo d'una Marcia (c).
          a. Melody with falling fifths is stated in the first violin, second
              violin, viola. Second section in C (meas. 29-61), with melody in
              the first violin, has an unusual rhythmic accompaniment in the
              piano and lower strings; cello joins melody (meas. 53).
          b. Return of the first theme is followed by an Agitato section in f;
              strong accents on the second beat of the theme; first theme ap-
              pears briefly with the triplet figure and tremolo accompaniment.
              Return of the second theme in F (meas. 133) and the first theme in
              c (meas. 165).
      4. Scherzo molto vivace (E-flat).
          a. Based on ascending and some descending scale passages. Form:
              Scherzo (meas. 1-45); Trio I (meas. 45-76); Scherzo (meas. 76-121);
              Trio II (meas. 122-195); Scherzo (meas. 196-239); Coda (meas. 239-
              264).
          b. Trio I (G-flat) has the characteristic falling fifth. The theme is
              in canon with the viola. Trio II (a-flat) makes use of the
              characteristic shift in accent. Short section in E returning to-
              a-flat; ascending scale passages through all instruments; Coda
              (meas. 240).
      5. Allegro, ma non troppo (c - E-flat).
          a. One of Schumann's best movements. Unusual skill is shown in the
              handling of contrapuntal material and in melodic invention.
          b. Sonata-form with unusual feature of two Expositions, two Develop-
              ments, and two Recapitulations.
              1) Exposition: first theme (c) (meas. 1-42); second theme (G) (meas.
                  43-77); closing section (b) (meas. 77-96). Development (meas.
                  96-136) uses the first and second themes. Recapitulation: first
                  theme (c-sharp) (meas. 136-178); second theme (E-flat) (meas.
                  178-212); closing section (g) (meas. 212-224).
              2) Exposition of third theme (E-flat) (meas. 224-248); Development
                  using parts of the first theme and a theme from the first move-
                  ment (meas. 248-378); Recapitulation of the third theme (E-flat)
                  (meas. 378-402); Coda is based on the first theme (meas. 402-
                  427).
          c. At measure 319 in the Development, the first themes of the last
              and first movements are used in a double fugue. This is an early

use of the device of bringing back material from earlier movements in the last movement (cyclic idea).
B. Quartet for Piano and Strings in E-flat, Op. 47 (1843).
   1. Followed the idea of his piano quintet. The Piano Quartet, however, is less brilliant; themes are often given to instruments in a weak register; the lower register is frequently used; the piano is often too prominent.
   2. First movement begins with a slow introduction which suggests the first theme of the following Allegro. First theme is repeated twice. Second theme (g) is accented on the second beat with the imitation between the piano and strings. Material from the Introduction begins the Development (d) which uses the first and second themes. Coda introduces a new theme (più agitato).
   3. Scherzo (g) is an extended movement based on one theme with two contrasting Trios.
   4. Andante cantabile (B-flat) reveals Schumann's melodic gifts. The melody begins after a three-measure introduction by the cello, which has the bass string tuned down from C to B-flat. The opening of the Finale is anticipated by characteristic falling fifths at the close of the movement.
   5. Finale (E-flat) begins with the interval of a fifth followed by a fugato section, announced by the viola. Cantabile second theme is introduced by the cello. A short subsidiary theme appears in imitation between the piano and viola. then cello and violin. The movement continues with the fugal theme in stretto; a new theme (A-flat) in the piano; a return of the fugato section.
C. Three Trios for Piano, Violin, Cello.
   1. Op. 63 (d) (1847); Op. 80 (F) (1847); Op. 110 (g) (1851).
      a. Characteristics include: sudden changes of mood; full harmony in piano with strings doubling outer parts; antiphonal effects; dotted note rhythms; compoun rhythmic figures; changes in tempo; syncopation; energetic movements; vague, formless movements; uneven quality; use of the falling fifth motive (op. 110).
D. Fantasiestücke for Piano, Violin, Cello, Op. 88 (1842).
   1. Romanza, Humoresque, Duet, March.
      a. One of the lesser works, with much use of doubling, sequence and a loose form.
E. Märchenerzählungen for Piano, Clarinet, Viola (1853).
   1. Four contrasting movements which lack vitality, but use interesting combinations of unusual colors.

BIBLIOGRAPHY
Books

1. Basch, V.   Schumann, a Life of Suffering. Transl. by C. A. Phillips. New York: A. A. Knopf, 1931. (ML410 S39B29P)

2. Bedford, H.   Robert Schumann, His Life and Work. New York: Harper, 1925. (ML410 S39B41)

3. Einstein, A.   Music in the Romantic Era. New York: Norton, 1947. (ML196 E35)

4. Evans, E.   Schumann. London: Novello, 1944. (ML410 S39E92)

5. Fuller-Maitland, J. A. Schumann. New York: Scribner, 1913. (ML410 S39F96)

6. Fuller-Maitland, J. A. Schumann's Concerted Chamber Music. London: Oxford University Press, 1929. (MT145 S39F96c)

7. Holloway, P. J.   <u>Use</u> <u>of</u> <u>Piano</u> <u>in</u> <u>Schumann</u> <u>and</u> <u>Shostakovich</u> <u>Quintets</u>.   ESM
      Thesis, 1946.

8. Mason, D. G.   <u>The</u> <u>Romantic</u> <u>Composers</u>. New York: Macmillan, 1926.
      (ML390 M39r)

9. Niecks, F.   <u>Robert</u> <u>Schumann</u>. New York: E. P. Dutton, 1925.
      (ML410 S39N66)

10. Peyser, H. F.   <u>Robert</u> <u>Schumann</u>, <u>Tone-poet</u>, <u>Prophet</u>, <u>and</u> <u>Critic</u>. New
      York: Philharmonic Symphony Society, 1948. (ML410 B39P51)

11. Reissmann, A.   <u>The</u> <u>Life</u> <u>and</u> <u>Works</u> <u>of</u> <u>Robert</u> <u>Schumann</u>. Transl. by A. L.
      Alger. London: G. Bell, 1908. (ML410 S39R3A)

12. Schuaffler, R. H. <u>Florestan</u>; <u>the</u> <u>Life</u> <u>and</u> <u>Work</u> <u>of</u> <u>Robert</u> <u>Schumann</u>. New
      York: Holt, 1945. (ML410 S39S31)

13. Schumann, R.   <u>Literarisches</u> <u>Verzeichnis</u> <u>der</u> <u>im</u> <u>Druck</u> <u>ershienenen</u> <u>Ton-
      werke</u> <u>von</u> <u>Robert</u> <u>Schumann</u>. By A. Dorffel. Leipzig: Fritzsch, 1875.
      (ML134 S392D)

14. Schumann, R.   <u>Thematisches</u> <u>Verzeichnis</u> <u>sämmtlicher</u> <u>im</u> <u>Druck</u> <u>erschienenen</u>
      <u>Werke</u> <u>Robert</u> <u>Schumanns</u>. Leipzig and New York: J. Schuberth, 1863.
      (ML134 S392.3)

15. Schumann, R.   <u>Music</u> <u>and</u> <u>Musicians</u>. Transl. by F. R. Ritter. London:
      Reeves, 1880. (ML410 S39R.2)

16. Storck, K.   <u>The</u> <u>Letters</u> <u>of</u> <u>Robert</u> <u>Schumann</u>. Transl. by H. Bryant.
      New York: E. P. Dutton, 1907. (ML410 S39S88B)

Periodicals

1. Davies, F.   "On Schumann - and Reading Between the Lines," <u>ML</u> 6 (1925),
      214.

2. Geiringer, K.   "Farewell of a Genius," <u>MusAm</u> 63 (1943), 24, 213.

3. Schumann, E.   "The Diary of Robert and Clara Schumann," <u>ML</u> 15 (1934),
      287.

Music

1. Wier, A. E.   <u>Miscellaneous</u> <u>Chamber</u> <u>Works</u>. New York: Longmans, Green
      & Co., 1940. (MT85 W64M67)

2. Schumann, R.   <u>Werke</u>. (Complete edition) 14 vols. Leipzig: Breitkopf
      & Härtel, 1883-93. (M3 S392)

<u>Individual</u> <u>Works</u> <u>or</u> <u>Groups</u> <u>of</u> <u>Works</u>

3. <u>Quartets</u>, Op. 41, Nos. 1-3. Miniature score. Leipzig: G. Eulenberg (A.
      Payne), 189-. (M452 S392.1-3mE)

4. <u>Quartets</u>, Op. 41. Parts. New York: International Music Co., 1944.
      (M452 S392QI)

5. <u>Quartet</u> <u>for</u> <u>Piano</u>, <u>Violin</u>, <u>Viola</u>, <u>Violoncello</u>, Op. 47. Score and separate
      parts. London: Augener, 191-. (M412 S392)

6. <u>Quintett für Pianoforte, 2 Violinen, Viola, Violoncell</u>, Op. 44. Score and
    Separate parts. Leipzig; Peters, 188- (M512 S392D)

		Records	
<u>Title</u>	<u>Music</u>	<u>Recording</u>	<u>Call No.</u>

I. String Quartets
    1. Op. 41, No. 1 (a)   W, 232   West 5166 (Curtis)

    2. Op. 41, No. 2 (F)   Lond 323 (New Italian)
                                      Col 4982 (New Music)

    3. Op. 41, No. 3 (A)   W, 244   West 5166 (Curtis)
                                        Col 4982 (New Music)

II. Piano and Strings
    4. Quartet, Op. 47   W, 275   Col 4892 (Horszowski, New York)
        (E-flat) (Piano,
        violin, viola, cello)

    5. Quintet, Op. 44 (E- W, 254   Vic 1095 (Rubinstein, Paganini)
        flat) (piano and   Col 4426 (Curzon, Budapest)
        string quartet)   Col 4711 (Hess, Stern)

III. Miscellaneous
    6. Trio No. 1, Op. 63 W, 287   Col 4718 (Horszowski, Schneider,
        (d) (piano, violin,   Casals)
        cello)   Dec 9604 (Mannes, Gimpel, Silva)
                                        Vic 1141 (Cortot, Thibaud , Casals)

    7. Trio No. 2, Op. 80   Vox 8480 (Bolzano)
        (F) (piano, violin,
        cello)

    8. Märchenerzählungen, Op.   West 5024 (Demus, Wlach, Weiss)
        132 (piano, clarinet,
        viola)

OUTLINE VIII
JOHANNES BRAHMS (1833 - 1897)

I. **Life.**

1833 Born at Hamburg, May 7. Studied music with his father, a double-bass player, and Marxsen.

1847 Made his debut as a pianist playing his own music.

1853 Accompanist for the violinist Reményi. Met Joachim and Schumann.

1857 Pianist and conductor for Prince of Lippe-Detmolds. Studied in Hamburg (1860-1862).

1862 Conductor of the <u>Singakademie</u> in Vienna (1862-64).

1864 Lived in Hamburg, Zürich, Baden-Baden, Vienna. Made concert tours. Met with increasing artistic and financial success.

1871 Conductor of orchestral concerts of "Friends of Music" (1871-74). Vienna became his permanent home (1878). Refused an honorary Mus. Doc. degree from Cambridge, but accepted a Ph.D. from the University of Breslau (1881).

1891 Visited Meiningen and heard the clarinetist, Richard Mühlfeld. He was so impressed with his playing that he decided to compose chamber music using the instrument.

1897 Died at Vienna, April 3.

II. **Catalogue of Chamber Music.**

A. String Instruments.
   1. Quartets.
      a. 3 for 2 violins, viola, cello.
   2. Quintets.
      a. 2 for 2 violins, 2 violas, cello.
   3. Sextets.
      a. 2 for 2 violins, 2 violas, 2 cellos.
B. Quintet for clarinet, 2 violins, viola, cello.
C. Piano with instruments.
   1. Sonatas.
      a. 3 for piano, violin.
      b. 2 for piano, cello.
      c. 2 for piano, clarinet.
   2. Trios.
      a. 3 for piano, violin, cello.
      b. 1 for piano, clarinet, cello.
      c. 1 for piano, horn, violin.
   3. Quartets.
      a. 3 for piano, violin, viola, cello.
   4. Quintets.
      a. 1 for piano, 2 violins, viola, cello.

III. **Chamber Music.**

A. Brahms wrote twenty-four chamber music works. His first chamber work was a Trio, Op. 8, for piano, violin, cello (1854). He restored the clarity of classicism and completed the classical school of Haydn, Mozart, and

72

middle period Beethoven. His forms are classical with an occasional suggestion of Romanticism. Twenty early quartets were destroyed before Op. 51 appeared (1873). Some early works were rewritten.

B. His themes are generally simple, but he invested them with great meaning. He used germ motives; themes evolving around one note; themes on successive notes of a chord (sometimes omitting one note); themes borrowed from songs. Motives from the subject were often divided between answering instruments. Themes are idiomatic for the instruments.

C. His harmony is based on the devices of the period: seventh chords, augmented sixths and triads predominate. Parallel thirds and sixths are a favorite device.

D. Complex rhythms are characteristic (2 against 3 and more involved combinations) and four-measure patterns are often avoided. Off-beat accents are frequent. His favorite rhythms are Dactylic (- ˇ ˇ) and Anapestic (ˇ ˇ -).

E. He favored traditional sonata-form, often treated in a highly dramatic way. He was a master of variation and used the rondo form in a variety of patterns. His third movements may be quiet or loud, but they are rarely capricious.

F. He frequently used many themes in polyphonic style, sometimes giving a thick texture to the music. Figurations in contrary motion and arpeggios are used in many ways. The cyclic idea is used.

G. His music is usually divided into four periods. He often worked on a composition for years with many revisions and destroyed all unfinished and unpublished MSS.
1. Early Period (up to 1855).
    a. Trio, Op.
2. Transition Period (1855-65).
    a. String Sextet, Op. 18.
    b. Piano Quartets, Op. 25, Op. 26.
    c. Piano Quintet, Op. 34.
    d. String Sextet, Op. 36.
    e. Sonata for Piano, Cello, Op. 38.
    f. Trio for Piano, Violin, Horn, Op. 40.
3. Mature Period (1865-90).
    a. Quartets, Op. 51, Nos. 1, 2.
    b. Piano Quartet, Op. 60.
    c. String Quartet, Op. 67.
    d. Sonata for Piano, Violin, Op. 78.
    e. Trio for Piano, Violin, Cello, Op. 87.
    f. String Quintet, Op. 88.
    g. Sonata for Piano, Cello, Op. 99.
    h. Sonata for Piano, Violin, Op. 100.
    i. Trio for Piano, Violin, Cello, Op. 101.
    j. Sonata for Piano, Violin, Op. 108.
    k. String Quintet, Op. 111.
4. Late Period (1890-95).
    a. Trio for Piano, Clarinet, Cello, Op. 114.
    b. Sonata for Piano, Clarinet, Op. 120, No. 1.
    c. Sonata for Piano, Clarinet, Op. 120, No. 2.

IV. String Quartets.

A. Op. 51, No. 1 (c) (1873).
1. A sonorous, dramatic work written on broad symphonic lines. The cyclic idea is used in the Romanze and Finale. First, Second, and fourth movements are based on two contrasting motives, rising and falling, which unite in a single idea.
2. Allegro (c). Sonata-form.
    a. 3/2 time. First theme in dotted quarter and eighth note rhythm

(meas. 1-10). The second theme is based on a falling motive (meas. 11-12). A third theme appears in measure 62 and a bridge section based on the first theme (meas. 83-86) leads to the Development (meas. 87-137). The Recapitulation (meas. 137) uses material similar to the Exposition and the movement closes with a Coda (meas. 227) based on the first theme.

3. Romanze, poco Adagio (A-flat).
   a. Related to the first movement by a dotted eighth and sixteenth rhythm. Effective use of the third relationship (C) (meas. 13-14). The middle section is in a-flat, with the characteristic use of empty first beats (meas. 27). First theme returns in the three lower instruments (meas. 49), followed by the middle section theme and a Coda using the first theme (meas. 86).

4. Allegretto molto moderato e comodo (f).
   a. The viola, one of Brahms' favorite instruments, is featured. Typical chromatic theme (meas. 15). The Trio (un poco animato) uses the "cariolage" effect in the second violin. Triplets in the passage marked "lusingando" (meas. 38) are combined later with the first theme (meas. 55).

5. Allegro (c).
   a. First theme is related to the first theme of the first movement. The second theme (meas. 70) has the same three notes as the first theme, but is in E-flat and in a quiet rhythm.

B. Op. 51, No. 2 (a) (1873).
1. Lyric style with contrasting passages. Earlier works for strings alone were two sextets. All movements are in A or a. Only Minuet in chamber works.

2. Allegro non troppo (a).
   a. Begins with a motto theme said to be Joachim's: (A)-F-A-E ("Frei aber einsam"). The second theme (meas. 46), in thirds and sixths, is one of Brahms' most attractive. Development is a compressed working our of measures 1-3. Recapitulation enters on the weak beat (meas. 183), preceded by the inversion of the F-A-E theme in the viola. Coda (meas. 287) introduces the motto theme in retrograde (meas. 323-328).

3. Andante moderato (A).
   a. In large A-B-A form. "A" section is in three parts (meas. 1-8(a); meas. 9-18(b); meas. 18-30(a¹). "B" section (meas. 43-76) is in two parts (meas. 43-60); meas. 60-76); second part is an elaboration of measures 1-8. "A" section (meas. 77-110) is a Recapitulation. Coda (meas. 111-124).

4. Quasi Minuetto, moderato.
   a. In Three parts. Much use of syncopation and cross accents. Part I is in three sections (meas. 1-16; meas. 16-28; meas. 28-40), all based on measures 1-16. Part II is a polyphonic Trio in 2/4, interrupted by a transitory passage, with two themes in canon. A transitory passage, again in canon, leads to Part III, a da capo (meas. 134). Coda (meas. 168).

5. Allegro non assai.
   a. Rondo with elements of sonata-form. Second theme (meas. 44); closing section (meas. 59-75); suggestion of opening theme (meas. 75-100). Development with suggestion of a Recapitulation (meas. 100-198); first theme (meas. 116); second theme (meas. 143). Recapitulation (meas. 198-293). Coda (meas. 293-359) uses the first theme in canon and a theme suggesting Schumann's Quartet in a (meas. 320), concluding with the first theme in diminution (Più vivace).

C. Op. 67 (B-flat) (1875).
1. Contrast to first two quartets. Full of humor; use of cross accents, syncopation, rhythmic counterpoint, hemiola rhythm.

   2. Vivace (B-flat).
       a. Sonata-form. First theme, in 6/8, is like a horn call. Hemiola
           rhythm (meas. 10-12); humorous stopping of theme on third eighth
           begins transition (meas. 21-31). Second theme group begins in
           measure 31. A third theme enters (meas. 58) in 2/4 time, which
           returns to 6/8 (meas. 60-63) and then to 2/4.
       b. Development (meas. 103-204), in 6/8 and 2/4 time. The material is
           largely derived from the first and second themes of the Exposition
           with change of signature from two flats to three sharps (meas. 127)
           and back again (meas. 161). There is a wide range of modulation.
       c. Recapitulation (meas. 205) is similar to the Exposition. The Coda
           (meas. 310) is a highly developed section which combines most of
           the previous material. The combination of 6/8 and 2/4 time ap-
           pears at the beginning of the Coda (meas. 312).
   3. Andante (F).
       a. Three-part form. Least successful movement of the quartet.
   4. Agitato (Allegretto non troppo) (d).
       a. Scherzo movement. The viola is prominent and the other instruments
           use mutes. Trio (meas. 130) is a neutral contrasting section. The
           final cadence is especially effective harmonically.
   5. Poco Allegretto con Variazioni (B-flat).
       a. One of Brahms' finest quartet movements. It consists of a folk-
           like theme with eight variations and Coda. All instruments take
           part in playing the three-part theme in its various shapes. The
           key changes give additional color. The first theme of the first
           movement returns in measure 95. Second theme of the first move-
           ment appears in measure 132. From measure 150 to the end, the
           triplet first theme and the variation theme are combined in various

V.   Two String Quintets.

   A. Op. 88 in F (1882) (2 violins, 2 violas, cello).
       1. Allegro non troppo ma con brio (F).
           a. First theme group (meas. 1-21) has a short contrasting section in
               D (meas. 9). The second theme, in triple rhythm, enters in the
               viola in A (meas. 9). It appears in the first violin (meas. 57)
               with the same two-against-three rhythm. Development (meas. 111-
               137) has an unusually long anticipation (meas. 111-137). Key
               contrasts of F and A are also used in the Finale.
       2. Grave ed appassionato (c-sharp) - Allegretto vivace (A).
           a. This movement is a combination of a slow movement and a Scherzo,
               with alternating Grave (c-sharp) and Allegretto vivace (A)
               sections. A remarkable passage begins with the theme in the
               cello (meas. 176), and the movement concludes unexpectedly in A.
       3. Allegro energico (F).
           a. Sonata-form with fugal sections. The brief fugue is followed by
               an augmentation of the first measure of the theme (meas. 23-26).
               The first three notes of the fugue theme become increasingly im-
               portant. The second theme in A (meas. 34) acts as a counter-
               subject to the fugue theme. Development (meas. 55) introduces
               (meas. 63) a chromatic theme, in triple rhythm and minor mode,
               which is derived from the fugue subject. Coda (meas. 146) uses
               material from the fugue subject, beginning with an expansion of
               the first three notes.
   B. Op. 111 in G (1890) (2 violins, 2 violas, cello).
       1. Allegro non troppo, ma con brio (G).
           a. An outstanding movement. The opening theme is in the cello. The
               bridge passage (meas. 21) gives prominence to the interval of a
               third. The second theme is in two parts (1st part. meas. 26; 2nd

part, meas. 38). There is a complex Development in five contrasting sections. Recapitulation (meas. 106). Coda uses the first
part of the main theme in the cello with the rising third motive
(meas. 162).

2. Adagio (d).
   a. The lyric main theme is treated without contrasting sections.
      Developed in G and reached a climx in D, returning to d at the Coda
      (meas. 69).

3. Un poco Allegretto (g).
   a. First section is a twelve-measure melody repeated. This melody is
      based on a falling second; sequential patterns. Second section
      (meas. 25) introduces a new motive, a rising third, which is imi-
      tated by the viola. Modulations lead through B-flat to g (meas.
      44). Trio (meas. 61) in G has a folk-like theme which is given to
      violas and violins alternately.

4. Vivace ma non troppo presto (G).
   a. A Hungarian peasant-dance Finale. The main theme is introduced in
      measure 13; second theme in measure 51. These tunes are used in
      many ways. The main theme appears in the final animato (meas.
      248).

VI. Two String Sextets.

A. Op. 18 in B-flat (1860) (2 violins, 2 violas, 2 cellos).
   1. The first of Brahms' published chamber works; some revisions were
      suggested by Joachim.
   2. Allegro ma non troppo (B-flat).
      a. Three principal themes: (1) meas. 1; (2) meas. 61; (3) meas. 107.
         The themes all have their own special rhythmic character. The
         second theme (meas. 61), in A, is in the style of a Viennese
         waltz.
      b. Themes are often suggested before they appear; modifications of the
         themes when repeated are a characteristic treatment (change from
         f-sharp to f-natural, meas. 76, 78).
   3. Andante, ma moderato (d).
      a. Theme and variations. This form is used six times in the chamber
         works.
   4. Scherzo (F).
      a. An unusually short, energetic movement in Beethoven style. Use of
         modifications of the theme (b-flat, meas. 45 - b-natural, Meas.
         49).
   5. Poco Allegretto e grazioso (B-flat).
      a. Rondo form. Main theme is in the style of Haydn, with the cello
         featured. Shows Brahms' skill in developing each phrase from the
         preceding one.

B. Op. 36 in G (1864) (2 violins, 2 violas, 2 cellos).
   1. Allegro non troppo.
      a. This sextet is lighter in texture, more profound, polyphonic and
         less complex than some of the preceding works and represents a new
         style development.
      b. Rising fifths at the beginning of the first theme are the basis of
         the whole movement. The viola repeats the notes g, f-sharp
         through the first thirty-two measures in spite of harmonic clashes.
         Development (meas. 217) uses a motive of fifths in all instruments;
         brilliant contrapuntal treatment; opens in d, modulates to the
         remote key of c-sharp.
   2. Scherzo (g).
      a. Three sections: Scherzo (meas. 1-120); Trio (meas. 121-250);
         Scherzo (meas. 251-371). Scherzo is also in three parts: Part I
         (meas. 1-33); Part II (meas. 34-68); Part III (meas. 69-120).

n   Material for the movement is derived from two motives (meas. 1-4; meas. 17-20). In measure 21 the cello plays the second motive accompanied by the first motive in inversion and with shifted rhythm. In measure 25 the two motives are combined again. Part II (meas. 34-56) has a motive generated from measure 31; uses a rest for the first beat. At measure 51, two motives are combined and developed in imitation. In measure 58, the return of the first motive is prepared in a major tonality. Trio (meas. 121) theme is a peasant dance; a contrasting theme (meas. 164) is derived from the Trio theme.

   3. Poco Adagio (e).
     a. This theme and variations is one of Brahms' greatest movements. Theme in three parts: (1) meas. 1-5; (2) meas. 6-8; (3) meas. 9-12). The variations are complex and frequently based on the harmony rather than the melody.

   4. Poco Allegro (G).
     a. Effective beginning out of the key, leading to broad cantabile melody (meas. 7).

VII. Clarinet Quintet in b, Op. 115 (1891) (clarinet in A, 2 violins, viola, cello).

A. This sextet is a great work, revealing Brahms' simplicity of material and his power to develop and give this material a meaning which is universal in its scope.

B, Allegro (b).
   al. First theme group (meas. 1-24). The second theme (meas. 37) is built on three notes of the scale: G, F-sharp, E. Development (meas. 71-135) uses the first motive; at the Quasi sostenuto (meas. 98) a bridge theme enters in D-flat; a rhythmic figure (meas. 99) is developed; modulations through B-flat, D-flat, A, F, C, to F-sharp (meas. 121). From measure 123, the rhythmic figure is answered in inversion. Recapitulation (meas. 136). Coda (meas. 195) begins with the first theme and the second theme motive is heard. The last twelve measures are one of Brahms' finest inspirations.

B. Adagio (B).
   1. Three-part form. Part II (meas. 52) is evolved from the first three notes of the first part. Rhapsodic, Hungarian-like treatment of the material. Part III (meas. 88) is almost like Part I. Coda (meas. 128) begins with a phrase on the clarinet, which is also derived from the first three notes of Part I.

C. Andantino (D).
   1. Strong contrast between the lyric Andantino (D) section and the Presto non assai (b). The staccato motive of the Presto is derived from the first four notes of the Andantino.

D. Finale, con moto (b).
   1. Theme and five variations. The theme of the first movement returns in measure 193.

VIII.Piano Quintet in f, Op. 34 (1864) (piano, 2 violins, viola, cello).

A. Originally written as a quintet with two cellos; rewritten for two pianos and finally as a piano quintet.

B. Allegro non troppo (f).
   1. Powerful first theme; bridge theme (meas. 23); second theme in the piano (meas. 34); concluding theme (meas. 74). Themes are usually prepared in the cadence of the preceding theme. Masterful treatment of a variety of rhythms.
   2. Recapitulation (meas. 166) is prepared in measure 160. Three-note motive without the first beat (meas. 248); first theme is varied and treated in imitation (meas. 261); first theme in the cello (meas.

271). Coda (meas. 283).
C. Andante, un poco Adagio (A-flat).
1. A-B-A form. A lyric movement, with a rhythmic melody in thirds and sixths; alternating between major and minor; rhythmic interest lies in the left-hand part and strings; first theme is suggested after middle section (meas. 55); return in measure 75.
D. Scherzo (c).
1. Strong rhythmic drive. Use of duple meter is unusual in chamber music Scherzos of Brahms. An example of unity with variety. Four themes, rhythmically contrasted, are used: (1) meas. 2; (2) meas. 13; (3) meas. 23; (4) Trio, meas. 194.
E. Finale (f).
1. Sonata-form without formal Development. First theme (meas. 42) follows the introduction and goes through many transformations in the course of the movement. Second theme (meas. 95). Concluding section is in syncopated triplets (meas. 138). A new version of the first theme (meas. 62) appears in c. Another variant (meas. 322) leads to the last transformation of the theme in the Coda (meas. 343). The second and first themes appear separately and in combination.

BIBLIOGRAPHY

Books

1. Anderson, W. R.   Introduction to the Music of Brahms. London: D. Dobson, 1949(ML410 B81A55)

2. Colles, H. C.   The Chamber Music of Brahms. New York: Oxford University Press, 1933. (MT145 B81C67)

3. Drinker, H. S.   The Chamber Music of Brahms. Philadelphia: Elkan-Vogel, 1932. (MT145 B81D78)

4. Evans, E.   Handbook to the Chamber and Orchestral Music of Johannes Brahms. London: W. Reeves, 1933-35. (ML410 B81E92Hc)

5. Fuller-Maitland, J. A. Johannes Brahms. London: Methuen, 1911. (ML410 B81F96)

6. Geiringer, K.   Brahms. His Life and Work. New York: Houghton Mifflin, 1936. (ML410 B81G31W).

7. Kilburn, N.   Chamber Music and Its Masters. New York: Scribner, 1932. (ML1154 K48.2)

8. Mason, D. G.   The Chamber Music of Brahms. New York: Macmillan, 1933. (MT145 B81M39)

9. Niemann, W.   Brahms, A Comprehensive View of the Man and an Exhaustive Critique of his Works. Transl. by C. A. Phillips. New York: A. A. Knopf, 1929. (ML410 B81N67P)

10. Schauffler, R. H. The Unknown Brahms, his Life, Character and Works. New York: Dodd, Mead and Co., 1933. (ML410 B81S31)

Periodicals

1. Abert, H.   "Bach, Beethoven, Brahms," MQ   (1927), 329.

2. Dunhill, T. F.   "Brahms Quintet for Piano and Strings, Op. 23," MT 72 (1931), 319.

3. Dyson, G.   "Brahms Clarinet Quintet Op. 115," MT 76 (1935), 315.

4. Fry, J.   "Brahms' Conception of the Scherzo in Chamber Music,"
     MT 83 (1943), 105.

5. Henderson, W. J.   "50 Years of Brahms," MusCo 106 (1933), 6 and 23.

6. Pulver, J.   "Chamber Music by Brahms in the Breitkopf Ed.," The
     Strad 44 (1933), 144 and 146.

7. Pulver, J.   "The String Music of Johannes Brahms," The Strad 43
     (1933), 28, 59, 99.

8. Robinson, E.   "The Interpretation of Brahms' Chamber Music," The Strad
     44 (1933), 305.

Music

1. Wier, A. E.   The Chamber Music of Brahms. New York: Longmans, Green
     & Co., 1940. (MT85 W64B81c)

2. Brahms, J.   Werke (Complete edition of the Gesellschaft der Musik-
     freunde in Wien). 26 vols. Leipzig: Breitkopf & Härtel, 1926-28.
     (M3 B81)

Individual Works of Groups of Works

3. Quartette, Op. 51 und 67. Separate parts; each Quartet bound separately.
     Berlin: Simrock, 1928. (M452 B81.1-3)

4. Quintets - Opus 88 and 111. Separate parts. New York: International Music
     Co., 1943. (M552 B813.1-2I)

5. Quintet for Clarinet (or Viola), 2 Violins, Viola, and Violoncello, Opus
     115. Separate parts. New York: Patelson, 1940. (M562 B813G)

6. Sextets, Op. 18 and 36. Separate parts. New York: International Music Co.,
     1943. (M652 B813.1-2I)

7. Sonatas for Violin and Piano, Op. 78, 100, 108. Scores and separate parts.
     New York: G. Schirmer (vols. 1301-3), 1918. (M219 B81K)

8. Sonatas for Cello & Piano, Op. 38, 99. Score and separate parts; each
     sonata edited separately. New York: International Music Co., 1947, 1943.
     (M231 B813.1-2)

9. Sonatas for Clarinet (or Viola) and Piano, Op. 120, Nos. 1 & 2. Scores and
     separate parts; each sonata bound separately. New York: International
     Music Co., 1948. (M250 B813.1-2I)

10. Trios (H-dur und c-moll) für Klavier, Violine und Violoncell, Op. 8, 101.
     Scores and separate parts; each trio edited separately. Berlin: Simrock,
     1926-7. (M312 B81.1 and 3S)

11. Trio in G Major, Op. 87. Score and separate parts. New York: International
     Music Co., 1946. (M312 B813.2S).

12. Trio in A minor, Op. 114. Score and separate parts. New York: International
     Music Co., 1946. (M322 B813.1I)

13. Trio in E-flat major, Op. 40. Score and separate parts. New York: International Music Co., 1946. (M322 B813.2SI)

14. Pianoforte Quartets, Op. 25 and 26. Scores and separate parts, each quartet bound separately. London: Augener, 19-. (M412 B81.1 and 2)

15. Pianoforte Quintet in F minor, Op. 34. Score and separate parts. London: Augener, 190-. (M512 B813A)

Records

Title	Music	Recording	Call.No.
I. String Quartets			
1. Op. 51, No. 1 (c)	W, 127	Col 4799 (Budapest)	
		West 5084 (Amadeus)	
		Lond 588 (Vegh)	
2. Op. 51, No. 2 (a)	W, 138	Cap 8163 (Hollywood)	
		West 5152 (Curtis)	
3. Op. 67 (B-flat)	W, 169	West 5152 (Curtis)	
		Col 4330 (Busch)	
II. String Quintets			
4. Op. 88 (F) (2 violins, 2 violas, cello)	W, 193	West 5027 (Vienna)	
5. Op. 111 (G) (2 violins, 2 ciolas, cello)	W, 216	Col 4711 (Prades)	
III. Clarinet Quintet			
6. Op. 115 (b) (clarinet, string quartet)	W, 240	Dec 9532 (Kell, Fine Arts)	
IV. String Sextets			
7. Op. 18 (B-flat) (2 violins, 2 violas, 2 cellos)	W, 22	Col 4713 (Prades)	
		West 5063 (Vienna)	
8. Op. 36 (G) (2 violins, 2 violas, 2 cellos)	W, 97	West 5263 (Vienna)	
V. Piano Quartets			
9. Op. 25 (g) (Piano, violin, viola, cello)	W, 39	Mer 10011 (Horszowski, Schneider)	
10. Op. 26 (A) (piano, violin, viola, cello)	W, 60	Col 4630 (Curzon, Budapest)	
11. Op. 60 (c)	W, 150	Col 4712 (Hess, Szigeti)	
		Mer 10010 (Horszowski, Schneider)	
VI. Piano Quintet			
12. Op. 34 (f) (piano, 2 violins, viola, cello)	W, 78	Col 4336 (Curzon, Budapest)	
		Cap 8269 (Aller, Hollywood)	
		West 5148 (Demus, Vienna)	

VII. Piano Trios
    13. Op. 8 (B) (piano,   W, 7   West 5237 (Badura-Skoda,
         violin, cello)   Fournier, Janigro)

    14. Op. 87 (C) (piano,   W, 180   Col 4720 (Hess, Szigeti,
         violin, cello)   Casals)

    15. Op. 101 (c) (piano,   W, 206   Alco 1025 (Compinsky)
         violin, cello)

    16. Op. posth. (A)   West 5058 (Holletschek,
         (piano, violon, cello)   Huebner, Harand)

VIII.Horn Trio
    17. Op. 40 (E-flat)   W, 116   West 5146 (Barylli, Koch,
         (violin, horn,   Holletschek)
         piano)   Col 4892 (Schneider, Jones,
                                               Horszowski)

IX. Clarinet Trio
    18. Op. 114 (a) (clari-   W, 230   West 5146 (Wlach, Kwarda,
         net, cello, piano)   Holletschek)
                                            Dec 7524 (Kell, Miller,
                                               Horszowski)
                                            Lyr 9 (Forrest, Greenhouse,
                                               Balogh)

OUTLINE IX

BEDRICH (FRIEDRICH) SMETANA (1824 - 1884)

I. Life

1824   Born in Leitomoschl, Bohemia, March 2. Due to his father's opposition, Smetana was largely self-taught in music.

1843   Went to Prague. Studied theory and piano with Proksch and gave music lessons.

1846   Took part in the Revolution of 1848 when Austria granted Bohemia political independence. Became strongly nationalistic. Received permission to establish a school of music, which he did with the financial help of Liszt.

1856   Went to Gothenburg, Sweden, as conductor of the Philharmonic Society. Composed tone poems.

1861   Returned to Prague and became active in the establishment of a national opera house. Composed a number of successful operas (The Bartered Bride, 1866).

1874   Resigned as conductor of the Prague opera because of political opposition and the strong criticism of his operas after 1868. He developed a nervous disorder and became totally deaf (1874). Turned to composition of symphonic poems (My Country, 1874-79) and wrote his famous string quartet in E minor, Aus meinem Leben ("From My Life").

1884   Died insane at Prague, May 12.

II. Chamber Music.

  A. Smetana composed only three chamber works: Piano Trio, Op. 15 (g), 1880; String Quartet (e) ("From My Life"), 1876; Second String Quartet (d), 1882.
  B. He is often referred to as the father of Bohemian music and was a leader in the development of a national school of composition. His music is descriptive, programmatic and always dramatic.
  C. String Quartet in E minor ("From My Life").
    1. Smetana, himself, explained the program of this quartet: I, his youth in the country, a fate motive; II, gay life in village and castle; III, a love scene, thoughts of his first wife; IV, his joy in work is interrupted by the tragedy of deafness, resignation.
    2. He said that the "four instruments should converse together in an intimate circle about the things which so deeply trouble me."
    3. Allegro vivo appassionato (e).
      a. Depicts his youth, love of art, romantic yearnings and a fateful warning of his future.
      b. Modified sonata-form. The agitated first subject (fate motive) is stated in the viola (p. 2, meas. 4). The romantic second subject (p. 5, meas. 23) is in G. The first four quarter notes of this subject furnish material for the following passages.
      c. Development begins (p. 8, meas. 1) with the first subject in the violin, answered by the cello. After a frenzied climax the music subsides (p. 11, meas. 5) and the first part of the second subject is heard in the cello.
      d. Recapitulation (p. 12, meas. 1) in E uses only the second theme. Fragments of the first and second themes appear in the Coda (p. 14,

> meas. 1).

4. Allegro moderato a la polka (F).
   a. Smetana wrote: "This movement recalls memories of my gay life in my youth when I used to write dance music and was known myself as an enthusiastic dancer."
   b. Rondo form: A-B-A-B-A-Coda. The "A" sections are in F and the "B" in D-flat. In the first "A" section a second theme is introduced in the viola (p. 18, meas. 1) and the first theme returns (p. 19, meas. 9). The first "B" section (p. 20, meas. 6) features a striking change in rhythm which Smetana said represented the aristocratic circles in which he lived.
5. Largo sostenuto (A-flat).
   a. Memories of his first love who afterward became his wife.
   b. Form A-B-A-B. There are two principal themes in this movement. The first "A" theme (p. 28, meas. 7), in the violin, is preceded by an expressive solo for cello (p. 28, meas. 1). The "B" theme appears in the violin (p. 31, meas. 9). After a cadenza for violin (p. 32, meas. 10) the first part of the "A" theme is heard, fortissimo, leading into the second "A" section with the theme in the cello. The "B" section is heard again in A-flat (p. 34, meas. 3) and the movement closes with a restatement of the "A" theme in the viola (p. 35, meas. 3).
6. Vivace (E).
   a. "Joy over the discovery of how to treat national material in music. Then the beginning of deafness and a glimpse into the melancholy future."
   b. The first group has two principal ideas, both strongly rhythmic (p. 36, meas. 1 and p. 36, meas. 9). The second theme, scherzoso, (p. 37, meas. 16) is used in various ways and leads to a return of the second idea,(fortissimo (p. 39, meas. 14). The scherzoso theme is used again (p. 10, meas. 18).
   c. Recapitulation (p. 42, meas. 16) presents the material of the Exposition with the scherzoso theme in the tonic (E). At the Più mosso (p. 45, meas. 7) the first idea is given to the violins in tenths, followed by an energetic statement of the scherzoso theme over a tonic pedal.
   d. After a two-measure rest, the mood changes abruptly (p. 14, meas. 14). An e"", sustained by the first violin over tremolo strings, represents the approach of Smetana's deafness. "There is a ray of hope, but with a sense of sadness." the second theme of the first movement is heard (p. 47, meas. 19). This theme alternates with the triplet figure of the first idea, pianissimo, as the quartet closes quietly.

BIBLIOGRAPHY

Music

1. Wier, A. E. Miscellaneous Chamber Works. New York: Longmans, Green and Co., 1940.

2. Aus meinem Leben. Quartett für 2 Violinen, Viola und Violoncell. New York: C. F. Peters, 1950. (M452 S63). Miniature score (M452 S63m)

3. String Quartet in E minor ("From my Life"). Wien: Wiener Philharmonisches Verlag, 192-. Miniature score (M452 S63mP)

4. Quartett, Zweites, für 2 Violinen, Bratsche und Violoncell. Berlin: Simrock, 1896. (M452 S63.2)

5. Trio in G minor (violin, cello, piano). New York: International Music Co.,

1943. (M312 S638I)

Records

Title	Music	Recording	Call No.
1. String Quartet in E minor (Aus meinem Leben)	W, 182	Str 613 (Stradivari) West 5199 (Curtis) Lond 865 (Vegh)	
2. Trio for Piano and Strings in G minor, Op. 15		Str 620 (Eidus, G. Ricci, Mittman)	

OUTLINE X

ANTONIN DVORAK (1841 - 1904)

I. Life.

1841　Born September 8 at Mühlhausen, Bohemia.

1857　Left home and entered the Prague Organ School where he studied with Pitzsch. He graduated in 1862 and joined the National Theatre orchestra as a violist.

1873　First important composition, Hymnus, was performed.

1875　Awarded the Austrian State Prize for his Symphony in E-flat and began intensive work in composition. Friendship with Brahms, Liszr and von Bülow helped secure performances.

1884　Visited England several times and conducted his own works. Awarded an honorary Mus. Dec. degree from Cambridge (1891).

1892　Became artistic director of the National Conservatory in New York (1892-95). Visited a Bohemian community in Spillville, Iowa.

1895　Returned to Prague as a professor at the Conservatory and became artistic director in 1901.

1904　Died in Prague, May 4.

II. Catalogue of Chamber Music.

A. String Instruments
    1. 8 String quartets (1874-95).
    2. 2 String quintets, Op. 77 (1875), Op. 97 (1903).
    3. 1 String sextet, Op. 48 (1878)
B. Piano and Strings.
    1. 4 Piano trios (1875-91).
    2. 2 Piano quartets, Op. 23 (1875), Op. 87 (1889).
    3. 1 Piano quintet, Op. 81 (1887).
    4. 2 Violin and Piano sonatas, Op. 57, Op. 100.
C. Dvořák composed a total of about thirty chamber works, including those in manuscript.

III. Style.

A. 1864-74.
    1. There is a strong influence of Beethoven and Schubert up to 1870. From 1870 to 1874 the influence of Liszt and Wagner predominates.
    2. Chamber works include five string quartets, one piano quintet, one string quintet.
B. 1874-78.
    1. Dvořák returned to the classic composers as his models.
    2. Chamber works include the string quartets Op. 16 (a), Op. 80 (E), Op. 34 (d), string quintet Op. 77 (G) (2 violins, viola, cello, bass), piano quartet Op. 23 (D), piano trios Op. 21 (B-flat), Op. 26 (g).
C. 1878-90.
    1. This period marks the beginning of strong Slavic elements in his music.
    2. A large number of chamber works were written, including a string sextet Op. 48 (A), string quartets Op. 51 (E-flat), Op. 61 (C), piano trios Op. 65 (f), Op. 90 (e), piano quintet Op. 81 (A), piano quartet Op. 87 (E-flat).

D. 1892-95.
   1. During this period Dvořák was in New York as artistic director of
      the National Conservatory.
   2. The string quartet Op. 96 (F), known as the "American Quartet" and
      the string quintet Op. 97 (E-flat) (2 violins, 2 violas, cello) were
      composed during his stay in America.
E. 1895-1904.
   1. He returned to Bohemia and wrote the quartets Op. 105 (A-flat) and
      Op. 106 (G).
F. Dvořák was a versatile and prolific composer with a gift for spontaneous
   melodic invention and a sense of form. He made use of national folk-
   tunes and rhythms and his works are frequently marked by strong emotional
   contrasts.

IV. String Quartet, Op. 96 (F), "American Quartet."

A. Written while Dvořák was visiting the Bohemian community in Spillville,
   Iowa.
   1. The work represents his impressions of folk music in America, but no
      authentic tunes are used.
B. Allegro ma non troppo (F).
   1. Sonata-form. A two-measure introduction is followed by the first
      theme which appears in the viola and then the violin. A subsidiary
      theme (p. 4, meas. 26) leads to the second theme (p. 5, meas. 11) in
      A.
      a. Development uses the themes of the Exposition. Recapitulation
         (p. 8, meas. 16) has the second theme in tonic (p. 10, meas. 20).
         An unusually short Coda concludes the movement.
C. Scherzo (F).
   1. This short movement is preceded by an expressive Lento (d).
   2. The Scherzo is based on two sections which appear five times in al-
      ternation I (F) - II (f) - I (F) - II (f) - I (F). The second
      section uses the theme of the first section in augmentation.
D. The finale, Vivace ma non troppo, is in rondo form with strongly contrasting sections.

V. Piano Quintet, Op. 81 (A) (1887).

A. The texture is generally harmonic and, possibly because Dvořák was a
   violist, the piano often plays a secondary role. The quintet is brilliant and colorful and his spontaneous melodic gifts are everywhere
   apparent.
B. Allegro ma non tanto
   1. Sonata-form. The quiet, expressive opening theme, alternating th
      between the tonic major and minor (last meas., p. 3) is given to the
      cello. A series of rapid modulations (C-e-B-e) on page 5 is followed
      by two statements, the first varied, of the first subject (p. 6, meas.
      10; p. 7, meas. 1). A transition (p. 7, last meas.) brings a sudden
      change of rhythm with a triplet figure and leads to the second theme
      (p. 9, meas. 7) in c-sharp. This melody is the basis of the remainder
      of the Exposition.
   2. The transition beginning on page 12, measure leads to the Develop-
      ment which opens with a figure in the bass. This is followed by a
      treatment of the opening of the first subject and the following
      passage, and the second subject. A striking passage (p. 20, last
      meas.) introduces the Recapitulation (p. 23, meas. 7).
   3. In the Recapitulation the second subject (p. 26, meas. 1) enters in
      f-sharp instead of the tonic key (A). The movement closes with an
      exuberant Coda.

C. <u>Dumka</u> (f-sharp).
   1. The <u>dumka</u> (pl. <u>dumky</u>), a Russian word meaning "thought," is a type of Slavic folk-song of elegiac character with strongly contrasting sections.
   2. This <u>dumka</u> is in a rondo form: A - B - A - C - A - B transposed - A. The contrasting sections are separated by double bars. Considerable rhythmic complexity appears in the <u>pochettino più mosso</u> section (p. 35) and the opening phrase appears transformed in the <u>vivace</u> section (p. 41).
D. Scherzo (Furiant) (A).
   1. A short sparkling movement with effective use of the high register of the piano (p. 56), three against five in the piano (p. 57), colorful modulation (p. 61, last meas.).
E. Finale (Allegro) (A).
   1. Sonata-form without repetition of the Exposition. The principal theme of the first subject (p. 70, meas. 12) is introduced by a theme which becomes an important part of the movement. The second subject, consisting of four themes, enters in the dominant (p. 75, meas. 2). The first subject appears just before the Development (p. 79).
   2. Development (p. 79, meas. 14) is founded principally on the first subject. A brief fugato appears (p. 83).
   3. Recapitulation (p. 86, meas. 1) begins with the principal theme of the first subject. The second theme is in the usual tonic key (p. 87, meas. 16) and a vigorous Coda concludes the movement.

BIBLIOGRAPHY

Books

1. Fischl, V., ed.   <u>Antonin Dvořák, His Achievement</u>. London: L. Drummond, 1943. (ML410 D988F52)

2. Hadow, W. H.   <u>Studies in Modern Music</u>. London: Seeley & Co., 1904-5. (ML390 H13)

3. Hoffmeister, K.   <u>Antonin Dvořák</u>. Transl. Newmarch. London: John Lane, 1928. (ML410 D988H71)

4. Robertson, A.   <u>Dvořák</u>. New York: E. P. Dutton and Co., 1947. (ML410 D988R64)

5. Sourek, O.   <u>Antonin Dvořák, His Life and Works</u>. New York: Philosophical Library, 1954. (ML410 D988S72)

6. Van Straaten, J.   <u>Slavonic Rhapsody: the Life of Antonin Dvořák</u>. New York: Allen, Towne and Heath, 1948. (ML410 D988V28)

Periodicals

1. Colles, H. C.   "Antonin Dvořák," <u>MT</u> 82 (April, 1941), 130; (May, 1941), 173; (June, 1941), 209.

2. Hadow, H.   "Dvořák's Quintet for Pianoforte and Strings," <u>MT</u> 73 (May, 1932), 401.

3. Hely Hutchinson, V. "Dvořák the Craftsman," <u>ML</u> 22 (1941), 303.

4. Hollander, H.   "Dvořák the Czech," <u>ML</u> 22 (1941), 313.

5. Lockspeiser, E.   "The Dvořák Centenary," <u>ML</u> 22 (1941), 299.

6. Nettl, P.   "When Dvořák Came to the New World," <u>MusCo</u> (Sept., 1941),
   5.

7. Newmarch, R.   "Anton Dvořák; a plea for remembrance," <u>Chesterian</u> (Jan.
   1923), 97.

8. Newmarch, R.   "The Letters of Dvořák to Hans Richter," <u>MT</u> 73 (1932),605.

Music

1. Wier, A. E. <u>Miscellaneous Chamber Works</u>. New York: Longmans, Green & Co.,
   1940.

I. String Quartets
    2. Op. 51 (E-flat). New York: International Music Co., 1943. (M452 D98.5I)

    3. Op. 61 (C). New York: International Music Co., 1949. (M452 D98.6I)

    4. Op. 96 (F) ("American"). New York: International Music Co., 1950.
       (M452 D98.7IT). Miniature score (M178 D98m)

    5. Op. 105 (A-flat). New York: International Music Co., 1948. (M452 D98.8I)
       Miniature score (M452 D98m)

II. String Quintets
    6. Op. 77 (G). Berlin: Simrock, 1888. (M552 D98.7)

    7. Op. 97 (E-flat). New York: International Music Co., 1943. (M552 D988.2I)

III. String Sextet
    8. Op. 48 (A). New York: International Music Co., 1943. (M652 D988I)

IV. Piano and Strings
    9. Quartet, Op. 87 (E-flat). New York: International Music Co., 1947.
       (M412 D988.2I)

    10. Quintet, Op. 81 (A). Berlin: Simrock, 1888. (M512 D98). Miniature
        score (M512 D98Em)

    11. Trio, Op. 65 (f). Berlin: Simrock, 1883. (M312 D988.2)

    12. Trio, Op. 90 (e).("Dumky"). New York: International Music Co., 1943.
        (M312 D988.3I)

Records

Title	Music	Recording	Call No.
I. String Quartets			
1. No. 3, Op. 51 (E-flat)	W, 36	Lond 387 (Boskovsky)	
2. No. 4, Op. 61 (C)		CH 1075 (Gordon)	
3. No. 6, Op. 96 (F) ("American")	W, 68	CH 1157 (Hungarian) Str 613 (Stradivari)	

	Dec 9637 (Koeckert) West 5199 (Curtis)
4. No. 7, Op. 105 (A-flat)	West 5337 (Barylli)
II. String Quintets 5. Op. 77 (G)	West 5026 (Vienna)
6. Op. 97 (E-flat)	Col 4799 (Katims, Budapest)
III. String Sextet 7. Op. 48 (A)	Rem 199-12 (Jilka)

IV. Piano and Strings
    8. Quartet, Op. 87
        (E-flat)
	Str 619 (Jahoda, Galimir)

9. Quintet, Op. 81 (A) W, 45	West 5337 (Farnedi, Barylli) Col 4825 (Curzon, Budapest) Lond 202 (Chigi)
10. Trio, Op. 65 (f)	CH 1117 (Kaufman, Cervera, Balsam)

11. Trio, Op. 90 (2)
     ("Dumky")
	Str 620 (Eidus, G. Ricci,
	  Mittman)

OUTLINE XI
CESAR (-AUGUSTE) FRANCK (1822 - 1890)

I. Life.

1822   Born at Liége in the Walloon region of Belgium, December 10. He be-
        came an accomplished pianist at an early age.

1833   Made his first concert tour of Belgium. Became a pupil of Reicha
        (harmony and counterpoint) in Paris (1835).

1837   Student at the Paris Conservatory with Leborne (counterpoint), Zimmer-
        mann (piano), and Benoist (organ). Received the "Grand Prix d'Honneur"
        for piano (first and only prize of the kind ever given); first prize
        for fugue (1840); second prize for organ (1841).

1842   Returned to Liége to begin his career as a composer; his father had
        wanted him to become a piano virtuoso. After two years in Belgium, he
        settled in Paris as a teacher (1844).

1851   Appointed organist of the church of St.-Jean St.-François.

1853   Choirmaster at Sainte-Clotilde.

1858   Appointed organist at Sainte-Clotilde, a position which he held until
        his death. Experienced the Siege of Paris (1870).

1872   Succeeded his teacher (Benoist) as professor of organ at the Paris
        Conservatory. Named a Chevalier of the Legion d'Honneur (1885).

1887   His works were presented at the "Franck Festival," sponsored by pupils
        and friends (Jan. 30). The program, directed by Pasdeloup, was well
        planned but poorly executed.

1890   He took part in the triumphal concert at Tournai with Eugène Ysaÿe. He
        was injured by a Paris omnibus while crossing a street, suffering com-
        plications which finally caused his death on November 8, 1890. Official
        coolness (marked during his life) continued after his death; neither
        the Ministry of Arts nor the Conservatoire sent a representative to the
        funeral.

II. Musician and Composer.

  A. A simple, modest, good, and warm-hearted man with a great capacity for
      work. He disregarded wordly considerations, displaying in his art the
      same strong faith as in his religion. His life was devoted entirely to
      teaching, composition, and playing the organ.
  B. He wrote a comparatively small number of important works and there is a
      wide difference in the quality of his music. Probably no composer of his
      rank was ever given so little recognition. His life was a consistent re-
      cord of neglect, coupled with badly-organized and technically inadequate
      performances.
  C. As a composer he was characterized neither by nationalism nor program
      music. After 1862, he stopped marking opus numbers; Op. 22 is the last
      one employed.
  D. The influence of his predecessors (Monsigny, Dalayrac, Grétry, Méhul) is
      shown in his early works - especially in types of melody and their treat-
      ments. At the same time, however, he used contemporary technics and was
      affected by developments of his time.
  E. Nineteenth-century French music was dominated by opera. Serious musicians,

dissatisfied, followed the path marked out by Franck. Among his pupils were Vincent d'Indy, Ernest Chausson, A. de Castillon, Pierre de Bréville, Charles Bordes, Guillaume Lekeu, Henri Duparc, Gabriel Pierné, Guy Ropartz, Augusta Holmes, Paul Vidal, Charles Tournemire - all of whom helped toward the establishment of a school of modern French instrumental music. Franck exerted a great influence at the Conservatory. His organ classes were also a training school for composers, who were grounded upon Bach and Beethoven.

F. His creative life has been divided by d'Indy into three periods: (1) 1841-52 (early works, trios, etc.); (2) 1858-74 (works largely of religious character); (3) 1876-90 (period of maturity and full possession of his artistic personality.

G. His music is characterized by contrapuntal excellence, formal innovations, religious idealism. He resembled J. S. Bach in his singleness of purpose and loftiness of ideals. His themes are apt to center around a pivotal note; he often begins a movement or section with a short figure which is repeated two or three times. He shows a fondness for keys with many sharps, seeming to attach a mystic significance to their use. He makes frequent use of a modulatory scheme with roots dropping a third and basses moving in chromatic lines. Cyclic form and the use of canons are characteristic.

H. The Schola Cantorum (founded in 1894 by Guilmant, d'Indy and Bordes) was organized to perpetuate Franck's influence and methods. After the death of d'Indy (1931), several members withdrew and began the École César Franck (1935).

III. Catalogue of Chamber Works.

A. Trios for Piano, Violin, Cello (1840).
1. Op. 1, No. 1 (f-sharp); Op. 1, No. 2 (B-flat); Op. 1, No. 3 (B).
2. Op. 2 (b).
B. Quintet for Piano, 2 Violins, Viola, Cello (f) (1878-79).
C. Piano and Violin
1. Andante quietoso (A) (1843).
2. Duo pour pianoforte et violon concertante (on themes from Dalayrac's Gulistan) (1844).
3. Sonata (A) (1886).
D. String Quartet (D) (1889).

IV. Trios for Piano, Violin, Cello.

A. The first three trios were written in 1840 and published later as Op. 1. They were dedicated to Leopold I, King of the Belgians, the presentation being made by the composer in person, but without any recorded reward. The influence of Beethoven is shown in Op. 1, No. 1; influence of Schubert and Weber in Nos. 2 and 3.
B. Trio Op. 1, No. 1 (f-sharp)
1. Cyclical form. Themes from the first movement are used again (somewhat transformed) in later movements. Other themes are derived from the main theme.
2. Andante con moto (f-sharp).
   a. Two themes, one the counter-subject to the other, are stated at the beginning (meas. 9) in the cello and piano. The counter-subject (piano) was used more than thirty years later as the cyclic theme in the Quintet for Piano and Strings.
   b. A third theme (meas. 83) completes the melodic materials.
   c. The movement is in five sections; themes "A" and "A^1" are treated in sections 1, 3, 4; theme "B" is merely stated (not developed) in sections 2 and 5.

    3. Allegro molto (b).
        a. Scherzo with double repetition is followed (meas. 213) by the
            first Trio (B), derived from the theme of the Scherzo itself. After
            the third section (a repetition of the first), a second Trio
            (being the expressive third theme from the first movement accom-
            panied by a rhythmic bass derived from the Scherzo theme) is in-
            troduced (meas. 411; combined meas. 472).
        b. In the fifth section (meas. 539), the cyclic theme "A^1" is com-
            bined with the Scherzo theme (meas. 557). The movement ends with
            an allusion to the second Trio and proceeds "attacca" to Finale.
    4. Allegro maestoso (F-sharp).
        a. The only movement in sonata-form. It is longer and more developed
            than the others. The opening phrase is a stirring version of the
            cyclic theme "A." Second theme (D-flat) is in Franck's religious
            mood. The movement follows regular formal lines, with the cyclic
            theme "B" triumphant at the end.
  C. Trio No. 2 (B-flat); Trio No. 3 (B).
    1. These works are inferior to the first Trio, both in material and
        musical interest.
    2. Franck called No. 2 (B-flat) a "drawing-room trio."
  D. Trio No. 4 (b) (listed by Cobbett as B major).
    1. Liszt, whom Franck met in Belgium, induced the rewriting of the final
        movement of the third Trio as a new, single-movement work. (Franck
        therefore supplied a new finale for No. 3.) It was published under
        the title of "Fourth Trio, Op. 2, and dedicated to his friend, Fr.
        Liszt."
    2. The work is original in form. The Recapitulation begins with the
        second subject.

V.   Quintet in f (1878-79) (piano, 2 violins, viola, cello).

  A. First performed in 1880 at the Société Nationale de Musique. One of the
    most popular of all piano quintets. In it the cyclic principle is car-
    ried to extreme limits.
  B. In the interval between the early chamber works and the Quintet (almost
    forty years), Franck slowly developed his unique harmonic style, with
    rich modulations and "chromatic wandering" as marked characteristics.
    The result was a type of writing best described as "restless and color-
    ful, but showing a somewhat loose harmonic structure." The Quintet is
    an example of this, at the same time demonstrating great economy of
    thematic resources.
  C. An expressive melody (cyclical theme of the entire piece) is used (in
    various forms) as the second theme and the Coda of the first movement,
    in the Development of the slow movement, and as the theme of the Finale's
    extended Coda. Each time it is altered in rhythm and tempo. This im-
    portant theme was in turn derived from one of the cyclical themes of the
    Trio No. 1 in f-sharp.
  D. Theme transformations are accompanied by sudden changes of mood and
    tempo, with modulations often being to remote keys (first movement in f
    presents the cyclical theme in the keys of E, G, f-sharp, A, D-flat).
    Tempo changes of "molto retardani" and "molto crescendi" are indicated
  E. Each of the three movements is in sonata-form, with an Exposition,
    Development, Recapitulation. In addition, the first and final movements
    have Introductions and elaborate Codas. Characteristics of the Franck
    style, however, make the music seem somewhat episodical.
  F. Molto moderato quasi lento-maestoso-allegro (f).
    1. The movement is built on two themes. After an introduction and
        statement of the first theme (meas. 50), which is derived from the
        opening phrase, a cyclic melody appears in several exploratory keys
        and is then finally announced in A-flat (meas. 124), thus taking the

function of a second subject. This second element is important in the
Development (meas. 143-269), appears in the Recapitulation (meas.
269-350), and in the Coda (meas. 350-440).
G. Lento, con molto sentimento (a).
　　1. Three themes are used in the three sections of the movement:
(1) opening "lento" theme, which is heard in the first violin, then
in other strings, and finally in the piano; (2) cyclic theme of the
Quintet (this time in D-flat, piano part, meas. 58); (3) a melodic
element which appears only during the exposition of the movement
(meas. 20), but reappears in the final movement as a second subject.
H. Allegro non troppo, ma con fuoco (F).
　　1. A movement of great brilliance. It opens with an introduction based
on fragments of the material to follow. First subject is fully announced by unison strings (meas. 73) and is followed (after a bridge
passage built on fragments of the same melodic element) by the second
theme (piano, meas. 147), which is derived from the second movement.
Development is built on the two themes. The first is treated rhythmically, the second is developed chromatically. At the end of the
Recapitulation the cyclic theme is heard again (by augmentation and
change of rhythm, meas. 388 in D-flat; meas. 404 in f in combination
with the first subject). A fast-moving Coda (meas. 430) closes the
movement and the work.

VI. Quartet in D (1889) (2 violins, viola, cello).

A. The last of Franck's chamber compositions. It was written only a few
months before his death, and the first performance took place April 19,
1890, at the Société Nationale de Musique.
B. Like the Quintet, D minor Symphony, A major Violin Sonata, this work is
based on a generating theme which supplies the complete musical material.
It is one of Franck's finest compositions and a high point in nineteenth
century French music, if judged for technical mastery, nobility of conception, and wealth of color. The idea of cyclical form is employed
probably more consistently than in any chamber music work since Beethoven.
C. Poco lento-allegro (D-d-D).
　　1. Combines two separate musical forms (each individual and complete) so
that the effect is one of a sonata-form inscribed within an A-B-A
form. The Exposition of the A-B-A in slow time is constructed of the
"germ motif" (meas. 1-6). The sonata exposition follows at once, with
the two transitional themes: "A" in d (meas. 61), "B" in F (meas. 138).
These two themes are connected by an important cyclic figure (cello,
meas. 105-106) which is much used in the Finale. At this point the
second part of the A-B-A appears (in place of the usual development of
the sonata themes), in the form of fugal entries of the original
"lento" element (meas. 174). Development (meas. 218), Recapitulation
(meas. 271) of the sonata exposition. The final section of the A-B-A
pattern follows (meas. 340).
D. Scherzo (f-sharp, F-sharp).
　　1. Characterized by feathery lightness; the use of mutes, and many measures of silence. There is a short quotation of the song-form of the
first movement (cello, meas. 225), after which the Scherzo is resumed.
E. Larghetto (B).
　　1. Less organic connection with the other movements. Extended aria form
in five sections: A-B-A-C-A. The fourth section contains references
to the Trio material in the preceding movement.
F. Allegro molto-larghetto-vivace (D).
　　1. Sonata-form. Begins with an Introduction which reviews themes of the
previous movements. The original "cyclic theme" of the first movement
is finally given a place of importance.

2. The Finale actually begins in measure 59. The "A" theme of the Exposition uses the opening of the "cyclic theme." The "B" part of the Exposition is a re-use of the bridge motif found in the Exposition of the first movement.
   a. This latter element is very important in the Development of the final movement. It is found first in augmentation (meas 113); then as adapted for a second subject in double augmentation (meas. 137). In this final form, it is a complete theme of three distinct parts (beginning meas. 137, meas. 193, meas. 237). Frequent changes of tempo and mood, added to a wealth of color achieved by modulations to remote keys, make this movement a striking one, a magnificent conclusion to the chamber music of César Franck.

BIBLIOGRAPHY
Books

1. Andriessen, H.   César Franck. Transl. from the Dutch by W. A. G. Doyle-Davidson. Stockholm: The Continental Book Co., 1947. (ML410 F82A57).

2. Demuth, N.   César Franck. London, 1948. New York: Philosophical Library Publications, 1949. (ML410 F82D38).

3. Mason, D. G.   From Grieg to Brahms. New York: The Outlook Co., 1902. (ML390 M39f)

4. d'Indy, V.   César Franck. Paris, 1906. Transl. by R. Newmarch. London and New York: John Lane Co., 1910. (ML410 F82I42)

5. Vallas, L.   César Franck. Transl. by H. Foss. New York: Oxford University Press, 1951. (ML410 F822V17)

Music

1. Quartet, D major. Leipzig: Peters, 1922. Separate parts. (M452 F822)

2. Quintette, F minor. Paris: Hamelle, 188-. Score and parts. (M512 F82)

3. Trio, F-sharp minor, Op. 1, No. 1. Leipzig: E. Eulenburg, 1930-. Miniature score (M312 F822.1m). Score and parts. New York: International Music Co., 1943 (M312 F822.1I)

Records

Title	Music	Recording	Call No.
1. String Quartet (D)	W, 125	Pol 1010 (WQXR) CH 1182 (Pascal)	
2. Piano Quintet (f) (piano, strings)	W, 141	Cap 8220 (Aller, Hollywood) West 5331 (Sokoloff, Curtis)	
3. Piano Trio (piano, violin, cello)		Vox 8950 (Bolzano)	

OUTLINE XII

GABRIEL-URBAIN FAURÉ (1845 - 1924)

I. Life.

1845 Born at Pamiers, Ariège, May 12.

1856 Studied at École de Musique religieuse with Niedermeyer, also with Dietsch and Saint-Saëns.

1866 Organist at St. Sauveur, Rennes.

1870 Assistant organist at St. Sulpice and organist at St. Honoré.

1896 Organist at the Madeleine. Succeeded Massenet as professor of composition, counterpoint and fugue at the Conservatoire. Became known as a song composer.

1905 Succeeded Dubois as director of the Conservatoire (retired 1920).

1924 Died at Paris, November 4.

II. Catalogue of Chamber Music.

A. 1 String Quartet, Op. 121 (1924).
B. 2 Piano Quintets: Op. 89 (1906); Op. 115 (1921).
C. 2 Piano Quartets: Op. 15 (1879); Op. 45 (1886).
D. 1 Trio for Piano, Violin, Cello, Opl 120 (1923).
E. 2 Sonatas for Violin, Piano: Op. 13 (1876); Op. 108 (1917).
F. 2 Sonatas for Cello, Piano: Op. 109 (1918); Op. 117 (1922).

III. Style.

A. Fauré occupies a unique place in the musical life of his native France. He was one of the first to break away from the Romantic School with its restricted harmonic idiom, and pointed the way toward greater harmonic freedom by the use of medieval modes. He represents the maturity of French chamber music and he influenced many French composers. Among his pupils were: Koechlin, Enesco, Schmitt, Ravel, Nadia Boulanger, Laparra, Roger-Ducasse. Fauré is probably best known through his songs. His chamber works constitute less than one tenth of his total output of over 130 works, but they are an important contribution.

B. Fauré represents a new post-romantic French style with some suggestions of the coming impressionism. His style is fluent, reflective, controlled, sensitive, elegant. He used augmented triads, chords of the seventh, ninth, eleventh, and thirteenth; appoggiaturas; planing; syncopation; whole-tone scales; irregular resolution of dissonances. Other characteristics of his style are the use of non-chordal tones in the bass, free treatment of inversions, rapid return to the key at a cadence.

C. His chamber music may be divided into the usual three periods. These periods are not based on radical differences in styles, but on the growth of the composer in freedom from influences of forerunners such as Gounod and Saint-Saëns, and also by an ever-increasing evidence of his own individuality as expressed especially through harmonic and melodic idioms and rhythmic unity.

1. First period (1876-1886) includes: First Sonata for Violin and Piano, Op. 13;. 2 Piano Quartets, Op. 15 and Op. 45.
2. Second period (1906-1921) includes: Piano Quintet, Op. 89 (announced earlier as Op. 60); Piano Quintet, Op. 115.

   3.   Third period (1922-1924) includes: Second Sonata for Cello and Piano,
        Op. 117; String Quartet, Op. 121.

IV.   Chamber Music.

   A.   Piano Quartet, Op. 15 in c (1879).
        1.   Allegro molto moderato (c).
             a.   Opens with a clean-cut, rhythmic theme. The three strings, in
                  their best range, are supported by the piano with syncopated
                  chords. Through a series of enharmonic changes the second theme
                  is arrived at in E-flat.
        2.   Allegro vivo (E-flat).
             a.   This Scherzo is a masterpiece of balance between piano and strings.
                  Use of staccato, pizzicato, syncopated rhythms and the character-
                  istic interval of the augmented fourth.
        3.   Adagio (c).
             a.   The opening theme in the cello is answered by theme in A-flat which
                  is reminiscent of Schumann.
        4.   Allegro molto (c).
             a.   Finale begins with Mazurka-like rhythms with occasional measures in
                  four-beat meter. There are three themes: (1) masculine;
                  (2) feminine; (3) based on a rhythmic pattern found in exposition.
   B.   Piano Quartet, Op. 45 in g (1886).
        1.   There are four movements, paralleling in construction and order of
             sequence those of the earlier Piano Quartet, Op. 15. This work shows
             a marked growth in the mastery of workmanship and in the individuality
             of the composer. The scherzo has the only use of the cyclic form to
             be found in his chamber music.
        2.   The strong impassioned opening theme is followed by a graceful second
             theme, which appears after being interrupted in its entrance by the
             main theme. A quiet third theme follows.
        3.   Allegro molto (c).
             a.   The Scherzo begins with a pizzicato accompaniment figure in the
                  strings. Both themes of the first movement are then used with a
                  change from binary to ternary rhythm.
        4.   Adagio non troppo (g).
             a.   Outstanding in rhythmic and melodic invention. The tonality wavers
                  between E-flat and g. A bell-like effect appears in the fifths
                  first sounded by the piano and later in the strings. The movement
                  closes with the distant effect of muted strings.
        5.   Allegro molto (g).
             a.   Finale is characterized by a marked conflict between the themes.
                  The rhythm, in triplet patterns, is first announced by the piano,
                  then by the violin and viola. The movement ends with the themes in
                  close stretto.
   C.   First Piano Quintet, Op. 89 in d (1906).
        1.   Allegro moderato (d).
             a.   The three themes of this movement are used with skill, although
                  the quintet as a whole is not one of Fauré's best chamber works.
        2.   Adagio (G).
             a.   Based on two themes. The first is in g in 12/8, stated by strings
                  with piano in triplets. The second is in b in 4/4 and treated
                  canonically. There is some use of chromaticism.
        3.   Allegretto moderato (D).
             a.   A scherzo-like movement. The theme in D is derived from a part of
                  the first theme of the first movement. This is contrasted with a
                  quieter theme in b. The form suggests a Rondo.
   D.   Piano Quintet, Op. 115 in c (1921).
        1.   Allegro moderato (c).
             a.   The opening theme is stated by the viola after one measure of an

arpeggiated accompanying figure in the piano. This is taken up by the other strings; cello, second violin (E-flat), first violin (c). The second theme is given out by the strings in the form of chords.

      b. Development involves canonic imitation between the strings and the piano. In the Coda an unusual harmonic effect is obtained by the alternation of the tonic chord (now in C) in its first inversion with it in root position as a tonic seventh chord.

  2. Allegro vivo (E-flat).

      a. The Scherzo is used for the first time since the Piano Quartet, Op. 45. There is an unusual alteration of scale passages throughout the movement. At the beginning the piano accounces a scale on E-flat which has a raised fourth degree, and also a passing chromatic C-sharp. In the third measure a Phrygian scale is used on E-flat. Modal treatment is used extensively.

  3. Andante moderato (G).

      a. The first theme is announced by the strings. The second theme is in the piano with a counter-theme in the upper strings as a descending scale in G.

  4. Allegro molto (c).

      a. The viola announces the first theme in two two-measure phrases. It then appears in immediate succession in the second violin, then in the first violin. The piano meanwhile supplies a bass which is accented in duple meter. The movement concludes in C with a very long passage in stretto.

E. Trio for Piano, Violin, Cello, Op. 120 in d (1923).

  1. Allegro ma non troppo (d).

      a. The opening theme is given out by the cello. Use is made of the characteristic interval of the fourth. The texture is thin and the melodies are simple, yet the effect is strong. Some use is made of the Lydian scale.

  2. Andantino (F).

      a. This fine movement is characterized by an expressive theme opening in the Lydian mode.

  3. Allegro vivo (d).

      a. Modulates through foreign keys without destroying the essential tonality.

F. String Quartet, Op. 121 in e (1924).

  1. Allegro moderato (e).

      a. Fauré's last work begins in a serious and melancholy vein and maintains an evenness of texture with little variety. The second theme enters in measure 35 and the Recapitulation in measure 111.

  2. Andante (a).

      a. This movement begins with a somber theme in the Locrian mode. Syncopation characterizes the rhythmic patterns.

  3. Allegro (e-E).

      a. Rondo form: A-B-A-C-B-A-B-A.

      b. A (meas. 1-41) - B (meas. 41-78) - A (meas. 79-116) - C (meas. 117-143) - B (meas. 142-163) - A (meas. 163-234) - B (meas. 234-260) - A (meas. 260-301) - Coda (meas. 302-312).

BIBLIOGRAPHY

Books

1. Koechlin, C. L. E. Gabriel Fauré (1845-1924). London: D. Dobson, 1945. (ML410 F26K770)

2. Suckling, N.   Fauré. New York: E. P. Dutton, 1946. (ML410 F26S94)

Periodicals

1. Chandler, T.   "Gabriel Fauré, a Re-appraisal," MM 22 (1945), 165.

2. Coeury, A.   "Gabriel Fauré," Sackbut 5 (March, 1925), 235.

3. Copland, A.   "Gabriel Fauré, a Neglected Master," MQ 10 (1924), 573.

4. Landormy, P.   "Gabriel Fauré," MQ 17 (1931), 293.

5. Orrey, L.   "Gabriel Fauré, 1845-1924," MT 86 (1945), 137.

6. Suckling, N.   "Gabriel Fauré, Classic of Modern Times," MR 6 (1945), 65.

Music

1. Wier, A. E.   Miscellaneous Chamber Works. New York: Longmans, Green
     & Co., 1940.

2. Quatuor à cordes, Op. 121. Miniature score and separate parts. Paris:
     Durand, 1925. (M452 F26)

3. Trio pour piano, violon et violoncelle, Op. 120. Score and separate parts.
     Paris: Durand, 1923. (M312 F26)

4. Quartet in C minor, Op. 15. Score and separate parts. New York: Inter-
     national Music Co., 1945. (M412 F265.1I)

5. Quatuor, 2me (sol mineur), pour piano, violon, alto et violoncelle. Op. 45.
     Score and separate parts. Paris: Hamelle, 18-. (M412 F26.2)

6. Quintette en re mineur, pour piano, deux violons, alto et violoncelle, Op. 89.
     Score and separate parts. New York: G. Schirmer, 1907. (M512 F26)

7. Quintette, 2me, pour deux violons, alto, violoncelle et piano, Op. 115.
     Paris: Durand, 1921. (M512 F26.2)

Records

Title	Music	Recording	Call No.
1. Quartet No. 1 for Piano and and Strings, Op. 15 (c)	W, 103	Poly 1007 (G. Casadesus, Guilet) Vic 52 (Rubinstein, Paganini)	
2. Quartet for Strings, Op. 121 (e)		Poly 1008 (Guilet)	
3. Quintet No. 2 for Piano and Strings, Op. 115 (c)		CH 1093 (Lev, Pascal)	
4. Trio for Piano and Strings, Op. 120 (d)		Mer 10089 (Albeneri)	

(ACHILLE-) CLAUDE DEBUSSY (1862 - 1918)

I. Life.

    1862 Born at St. Germain-en-Laye, August 22.

    1873 Entered the Conservatoire at Paris after studies with Mme. de Fleur-
         ville, a pupil of Chopin. Studied piano with Marmontel, solfeggio with
         Lavignac, harmony with E. Durand.

    1880 Met Tschaikowsky's patroness, Mme. von Meck and travelled with her in
         Italy, Switzerland, Austria, Russia. Influenced by Mme. Vasnier, a
         singer, to whom he dedicated Fêtes galantes on poems of Verlaine.

    1884 Won the Grand Prix de Rome with his cantata L'Enfant prodigue. Wrote
         La Damoiselle élue (1887).

    1892 Wrote L'Après-midi d'un Faune; began Pelléas et Mélisande; String
         Quartet (1893).

    1901 Trois Nocturnes (Nuages, Fêtes, Sirènes). Dedicated to his first wife
         Rosalie Texier. In 1904 he married Mme. Emma Bardac.

    1904 La Mer completed in England. Images (1906).

    1908 Conducted own works in London, Paris, Vienna, Budapest, Turin, Moscow,
         St. Petersburg, Amsterdam, Rome.

    1914 Planned an American tour with Arthur Hartmann, but gave it up because
         of ill health.

    1918 Died at Paris, March 25, of cancer.

II. Catalogue of Chamber Music.

    A. String Quartet (1893).
    B. Rapsodie for saxophone and piano (1903-05).
    C. Première rapsodie for clarinet and piano (1909-10).
    D. Sonata for Violoncello (1915).
    E. Sonata for Flute, Violin, Harp (1915).
    F. Sonata for Violin and Piano (1916-17).

III. Style.

    A. Debussy developed a new style in music known as Impressionism. It began
        as a revolt against dynamic, logical German classicism and the extrava-
        gant emotionalism of romanticism. Paintings of the French Impressionists
        Monet and Renoir, and the refined poetry of Verlaine (1844-96), Mallarmé
        and others suggested a new type of music, essentially French in nature.
    B. Although the first great composer of "New Music" of the twentieth cent-
        ury, Debussy is sometimes said to represent the final culmination of
        romanticism. His musical style was evolved from elements found in the
        music of Franck, Wagner (whose music he disliked). Borodin, Mousso rgsky.
        He was also influenced by the delicacy and poetry of Chopin and the
        rhythms and colors of Javanese music.
    C. Impressionism is concerned with sonority; the play of tone colors; tran-
        sitory impressions and sensations; the veiled rather than the obvious;
        the translation of poetry into music; unusual and striking instrumental
        colors and harmonies; form based on the mood and color of the sections.

D. Characteristics of harmonic style.
  1. Usually there is one principal part, which is colored by chords; real part-writing is rarely if ever used.
  2. Chords in parallel motion ("planing").
  3. Melodic lines are short and are often used as motives.
  4. Whole-tone scales are sometimes used in melodies and chordal combinations, including tritones and augmented intervals. Chromatic lines are used for special effects.
  5. Modes are used; sometimes one mode is used melodically while another is used harmonically (major, minor or church modes).
  6. Frequent use of common chords in unusual successions; seventh chords and triads; triads with added seconds, fourths, sixths, sevenths; augmented fourths.
  7. Unresolved dissonances. Freedom on modulation, often enharmonic.
  8. Key changes of third, second, fifth relationships. Rapid changes in harmony occur.

IV. Chamber Music.

  A. Première Quatuor, Op. 10 (g) (1893).
    1. Chamber music represents only a small part of his compositions. His first chamber music work, the Quartet (1893),does not break completely with the past, but the general effect is entirely unlike other music. There is some use of the principles of development; repetition; a little imitation; sequence modulations; rhythmic transformations; cyclic treatment. About one-half of the chords are sevenths, over one-third are triads. Most of the rest are ninth chords, with a very few eleventh and thirteenth chords. Seventh chords often have the close (dissonant) intervals at the bottom, which accentuates the dissonance. The seventh is approached and left freely.
    2. Animé et très décidé (g).
      a. Sonata-form with more than the usual number of themes. The generating theme (A), in Phrygian mode, appears frequently throughout the movement, somewhat like a Wagnerian leit-motif.
      b. Exposition: A - B (p. 1, meas. 13) - A (p. 3, meas. 2) - C (2nd theme, p. 3, meas. 15) - D (p. 4, meas. 12).
      c. Development: A (p. 5, meas. 10) - E (sometimes called 2nd theme, p. 5, meas. 12) - A - E - A - E - A.
      d. Recapitulation: A (p. 11, meas. 8) - F (p. 12, meas. 7) - E (p. 13, meas. 6) - H (p. 14, meas. 2) - E (p. 14, meas. 8) - Coda (p. 15, meas. 4).
    3. Assez vif et bien rythmé (G).
      a. Form is basically A - B - A - B (developed) - Coda. Material is mostly derived from the generating theme "A." Much use of pizzicato.
      b. Generating theme "A" is presented in a Scherzo mood by the viola (p. 16, meas. 3) with many repetitions. A subsidiary theme appears in the first violin (p. 16, meas. 9). Theme "A" is in the first violin (p. 17, meas. 17) and cello (p. 18, meas. 7).
      c. Theme "B" (2nd theme) is an augmentation of Theme "A" (p. 18, meas. 16).
      d. Theme "A" is in the viola (p. 20, meas. 11), second violin (p. 21, meas. 2), first violin (p. 21, meas. 8).
      e. Theme "B" (p. 21, meas. 19) is developed with altered rhythms and varied tonalities.
      f. Coda (15/8 time) begins with a modified version of the "A" theme in the viola (p. 24, meas. 6). It concludes with the tremolo figure used to introduce the "B" theme (p. 18, meas. 14).
    4. Andantino, doucement expressif (D-flat).
      a. Generating theme "A" is only remotely connected, if at all, with

this movement. The lyrical feeling in the melody recalls the slow movement of Borodin's First Symphony.

b. Form: A - B - C (developed) - B - A. Relation of theme "C" to "B" results in a feeling of ternary form.

c. Theme "A" appears after the "motto" beginning (p. 27, meas. 1-4). Mutes are used in all four instruments. Characteristic Debussy harmonies are found in measure 15, p. 27.

d. Second section (p. 28, meas. 13) is introduced by theme "B" (or 2nd theme) in viola, which is varied in the following measure.

e. Theme "C", an extension of theme "B," enters in the viola (meas. 12, p. 29). This theme then appears in the cello (p. 29, meas. 19); in octaves with the cello and second violin (p. 30, meas. 4). The use of a whole-tone scale (accompanied by thirds). and the resulting augmented triads, is characteristic of many later works. The climax of the movement is reached in measures 1-4, page 31. Development of theme "C" continues with the use of part of the theme, repetition, and sequence. A last statement of the first part of the theme in solo cello (p. 31, meas. 16) is introduced by a whole-tone scale.

f. Theme "B" returns, stated in octaves (p. 31, meas. 20), and the solo cello modulates back to theme "A."

5. Très modéré (D-flat, G).

a. Form: Introduction - A - B - A - C - Coda. Theme "C" is the generating theme.

b. Introduction (p. 33-35, meas. 1-30). Theme "C" is used in altered form and appears in imitation (p. 33, meas. 15-20). The theme is divided between the cello and viola (p. 34, meas. 4-7) and then appears in octaves between the viola and the first violin, accompanied by the second violin and cello in octaves (p. 34, meas. 8-9). The Introduction ends on page 35 at measure 30.

c. Finale actually begins with the très mouvementé (p. 35). The "A" theme is in the viola (p. 35, meas. 4-5). There is a suggestion of the generating theme "C" in the first and second violins (p. 35, meas. 18 - p. 36, meas. 5). Theme "A" returns on page 36, measures 7-8.

d. Theme "B" is derived from the second measure of theme "A." Theme "B" is divided between the violin and viola (p. 36, meas. 11-12). It is used in sequence and as a repeated rhythmic figure in the viola. It then appears in the first violin (p. 36, meas. 21). The transition to theme "A" (p. 38, meas. 1 - p. 39, meas. 3) uses fragments of "A" in augmentation in the cello (p. 38, meas. 8), and in octaves between the cello and violin (p. 38, meas. 16-19). The second measure of theme "A" is altered and in augmentation (p. 38, meas. 29 - p. 39, meas. 3). Theme "A" is in octaves, accompanied by chromatic lines in octaves (p. 39, meas. 4-7).

e. Theme "C" (2nd theme), the generating theme, is used in augmentation, accompanied by a rhythmic ostinato from theme "A" (p. 39, meas. 15); in augmentation and syncopated (p. 40, meas. 10); in a triplet figure in the viola (p. 40, meas. 14) and later in the second violin. Theme "A" in the first violin is combined with the augmented theme "C" in the second violin (p. 41, meas. 14-18), then in the second violin and viola (p. 42, meas. 11) and extended (p. 43).

f. Theme "A" appears again (p. 44, meas. 8) and the two parts of theme "A" are used in various ways. Theme "B" is used in augmentation in the cello (p. 45, meas. 1-5). Theme "A" is in octaves (p. 45, meas. 10). The second part of theme "A" appears in augmentation (p. 45, meas. 11-12).

g. Theme "C" is varied in the second violin and viola (p. 45, meas. 13). There is some use of imitation (p. 45, meas. 17-20).

Themes "C," "A," and "B" are varied (p. 46, meas. 1 - p. 47, meas. 17). Theme "C" is in augmentation in the second violin (p. 48, meas. 1) and extended in the first violin (p. 48, meas. 10). Coda begins on page 49, measure 11.

 h. Coda (p. 49, meas. 11) is based on generating theme "C" as it appears in the Scherzo movement. Theme "B" is in the cello (p. 49, meas. 19). Triplet figure of the theme (augmented, p. 50, meas. 14) leads to a brilliant conclusion.

B. Sonata for Flute (Violin), Viola, Harp (1916).

 1. Pastorale, Interlude, Finale. The themes of the movements are all closely related. The entire work is rhythmically complex.

 2. The form of the first movement is ternary. There are five short, arabesque-like themes and polytonality is suggested. The bright Interlude is marked "Tempo di Minuetto" and the last movement is rapid and rhythmic.

BIBLIOGRAPHY

Books

1. Calvocoressi, M. D. *Debussy.* London: Novello & Co., 1940. (ML410 D28C16)

2. Debussy, C. *Monsieur Croche, the dilettante hater.* Transl. by B. N. Langdon Davies. New York: Lear Publishers, 1948. (ML60 D28MD)

3. Dumesnil, M. *Claude Debussy, Master of Dreams.* New York: I. Washburn, 1940. (ML410 D28D88).

4. Dumesnil, M. *How to Play and Teach Debussy.* New York: Schroeder & Gunther, 1932. (MT145 D28D88)

5. Harvey, H. B. *Claude of France, the story of Debussy.* New York: Allen, Town & Heath, 1948. (ML410 D28H34)

6. Ketting, P. *Claude-Achille Debussy.* Transl. by W. Doyle-Davidson. Stockholm: Continental Book Co., 1947. (ML410 D28K43)

7. Lockspeiser, E. *Debussy.* New York: E. P. Dutton, 1936. (ML410 D28L81)

8. Mason, D. G. *Contemporary Composers.* New York: Macmillan, 1918. ML390 M39C)

9. Shera, E. H. *Debussy and Ravel.* New York: Oxford University Press, 1927. (MT92 D28S55)

10. Thompson, O. *Debussy, Man and Artist.* New York: Dodd, Mead & Co., 1937. (ML410 D28T47)

11. Vallas, L. *Claude Debussy, His Life and Works.* Transl. by G. O'Brien. New York: Oxford University Press, 1933. (ML410 D28V17CO)

12. Vallas, L. *The Theories of Claude Debussy.* Transl. by G. O'Brien. New York: Oxford University Press, 1929. (ML410 D28V17Q)

Periodicals

1. Bauer, H. "Recollections of Debussy," *Musician* (Feb., 1931), 21.

2. Cohen, A. "Debussy's Poets Translated," *ML* 18 (1937), 158.

3. Dumesnil, M.   "Claude Debussy as a Music Critic," Etude (April, 1946),
        203.

4. Franco, J.   "Debussy as a Melodist," MusAm 60 (Nov., 1940), 5.

5. Lavauden, T.   "Humour in the Work of Debussy," Chesterian 9 (1928),
        183, 209.

6. Lockspeiser, E.   "Debussy During the Last War," MusAm (Feb. 10, 1941), 227.

7. Lockspeiser, E.   "Some Projects of Debussy," Chesterian 17 (1935), 11.

8. Mellers, W. H.   "The Final Works of Claude Debussy," ML 20 (1939), 168.

9. Molie, D.   "Apropos of the Interpretation of Claude Debussy," Golus
        8 (1929), 13.

10. Palache, J. G.   "Debussy as Critic," MQ 10 (1924), 361.

11. Phillips, C. H.   "The Symbolists and Debussy," ML 13 (1932), 298.

12. Revue Musicale (La) December, 1920, entire issue. (French)

13. Sabaneev, L.   "Claude Debussy," ML 10 (1929), 1.

14. Ternant, A.   "Debussy and Brahms," MT 65 (1924), 608.

Music

1. Wier, A. E.   Miscellaneous Chamber Works. New York: Longmans, Green
        & Co., 1940.

2. String Quartet, Op. 10. Miniature score and parts.   New York: E. F. Kalmus,
        193- and 194-. (M452 D289K)

3. Six Sonatas pour Divers Instruments. Score and separate parts, each bound
        separately. Paris: Durand, 1915.

Records

Title	Music	Recording	Call No.
1. String Quartet, Op. 10 (g)	W, 21	Col 4668 (Budapest) Phil 104	
2. Sonata for Flute, Viola, Harp		West 5207 (Wanausek, Weiss, Jellinek)	

MAURICE (JOSEPH) RAVEL (1875 - 1937)

I. **Life.**

1875   Born at Ciboure, Basses-Pyrénées, March 7. His family moved to Paris
       when he was three months old. He studied piano with H. Ghis (1882)
       and later, harmony with Charles-René.

1889   Entered the Conservatoire, where he studied with Ch. de Bériot and
       E. Pessard. He began to compose and became a pupil of Fauré (1897)
       and Gédalge. His artistic personality was revealed in his first
       works.

1899   Made his début as conductor. He won the second Prix de Rome (1901)
       with his cantata Myrrha, but failed to win first prize in three
       attempts.

1905   In spite of academic hostility and the accusation that he imitated
       Debussy, Ravel continued to compose in his own highly individual
       manner. Daphnis et Chloe (1909-11) definitely established his reputa-
       tion.

1916   Drove an ambulance at front during World War I (1916-17). Appeared as
       pianist and conductor and was in America and Canada (1928). Received
       a Mus.Doc. degree from Oxford University (1928), but refused the
       Legion of Honor. Ralph Vaughan Williams was one of his few pupils.

1930   Last important compositions were two piano concertos, one for left
       hand alone (1930-31). He suffered from a cerebral disorder and was
       unable to compose after 1933.

1937   Died at Paris, Dec. 28.

II. **Catalogue of Chamber Music.**

A. Quartet in F Major (1902).
B. Introduction and Allegro for Harp solo, Flute, Clarinet, String Quartet
    (1906).
C. Three Poems of Stephane Mallarmé for Voice, Piccolo, Flute, 2 Clarinets,
    String Quartets (1913).
D. Trio in A minor for Violin, Cello, Piano (1915).
E. Sonata for Violin, Cello (1920-22).
F. Berceuse on the name of Fauré for Violin, Piano (1922).
G. Sonata for Violin, Piano (1923-27).

III. **Style.**

A. Ravel was influenced during his early years by Spanish and Russian
    (Rimsky-Korsakow) music, and later by his French contemporaries Satie
    (opposed to Wagnerian style), Chabrier (lively melodies and rhythms,
    clear orchestration) and Saint-Saëns.
B. His melodic lines are clear and sometimes modal. There is much use of
    seventh, eleventh, and thirteenth chords; small intervals, bold harmonies;
    unresolved dissonances; non-harmonic tones; many appoggiaturas instead of
    traditional resolutions.
    1. Long pedals, sometimes inverted, are used. Tonality is retained, al-
        though it may be modal or even polymodal. Modal melodies usually
        have a major harmonic background.

2. The whole-tone scale and chromatic progressions are avoided.
C. Rhythms are subtle, bright, frequently changing, but rarely complicated.
They are generally strong and straight-forward in comparison with many of
his contemporaries.
    1. He does not sacrifice clarity of outline for "impressionistic" effects,
and the development of the poetic idea is the first consideration.
D. Form follows the classical conception. Cyclic treatment is found in almost all works. The scoring is clean and colorful and very resonant
considering the small groups employed. There is frequent repetition of
phrases.
E. His music is sensitive and colorfully and carefully designed. It is
never sentimental.
    1. Although considered to be a follower of Debussy, Ravel has a style
which is original and individual. General similarities in the
quartets of Ravel and Debussy include cyclic treatment, use of
pizzicati in the second movement and mutes in the third movement. The
two composers are, however, different as regards materials and
methods.

IV. Quartet in F (1902). Dedicated to Fauré.

A. The entire quartet shows great originality, and mature technique in
handling and exploiting both melodic line and harmonic progression. It
is never contrapuntal in the imitative sense, but has contrasting melodic
lines running simultaneously.
B. Allegro Moderato (F).
    1. Sonata-form. Exposition has the first theme in F, the second in d
(p. 4, meas. 9). Development (p. 5, meas. 69) begins with the second
part of the second theme in B-flat. The first theme is varied in the
second violin (p. 5, meas. 8). The second part of the Development
begins on page 6, measure 1. Recapitulation (p. 9) begins in F, and
after a number of tonality changes, the second theme appears in F
(p. 12, meas. 5). Transition to the Coda (mea. 199).
    2. Melodically, the form is very clear. Harmonically, the analysis is
more complex because of numerous appoggiaturas and appearances of incomplete ninth and eleventh chords. These chords are often voiced
with a close spacing between the middle voices. The chief melodic
interest is carried either by the first violin or the viola, with an
occasional appearance in the second violin. The use of tremolo is
frequent throughout the entire quartet, and also the characteristic
repetitions of short phrases.
C. Assez vif - Très rythmé (a).
    1. A scherzo movement, with interesting use of pizzicato. It is based on
two contrasting themes. The first theme is in the Aeolian mode.
Second theme (p. 14, meas. 13). There is much use of cross-rhythms.
Development uses both themes in various tonalities, with many rhythmic
and tempo changes. Recapitulation of the first section begins on page
23, measure 7.
D. Très lent (a - G-flat).
    1. In fantasy style. Three contrasting themes. The second theme (p. 26,
meas. 19) is related to the main theme of the first movement. There
are many changes of tempo and meter; use of mutes. Arpeggios and
tremolos are used as an accompaniment figure.
E. Vif et agité (F).
    1. Form: A-B-C-A-B-A-C-B-C-A-Coda. The movement begins with a rapid 5/8
in unison. A 5/4 bridges this into the "B" theme (p. 36, meas. 12)
which, although written in 3/4, gives no feeling of bar-lines. The
"B" theme is based on the first theme of the first movement. Theme
"C" (p. 37, meas. 18) is derived from the second theme of the first
movement.

V. Introduction et Allegro (G-flat) (1908).

    A. Scored for harp solo, flute, clarinet, string quartet. The first theme (introduction) is in parallel thirds between the flute and clarinet. The second theme is given to strings in three parallel octaves (meas. 3-6). The cello, in a slightly faster passage, introduces the third theme with and arpeggiated accompaniment for strings and winds.

    B. In the Allegro, the harp develops the second theme without accompaniment by the other instruments. This is followed by a tutti statement of the same theme. The harp joins the group again and the theme alternates between the flute and clarinet. After a short harp cadenza, the flute and clarinet present a new theme (fifth theme) in octaves. The first theme returns in muted strings, followed by a slightly altered version of the second theme in the harp. A rhapsodic section, using the fifth theme, follows. The second theme joins it twenty measures after a harp cadenza. These themes work towards the most extensive harp cadenza of the piece. The second theme appears in the harp after the cadenza. Following the development of the second theme, the fifth theme returns and is built up to a brilliant conclusion.

VI. Trio in a for Violin, Cello, Piano (1915).

    A. Modéré.
       1. The piano gives the first statement of the theme. The violin and cello then join, two octaves apart. The second theme is slower and contrasting.

    B. Pantoum.
       1. The colors of the violin are exploited by the use of pizzicato, arco, harmonics, double stops - all in four measures. The piano takes an active part in the ensemble and is not an accompanying instrument. The piano exploits the Ravel characteristic of presenting a complete thematic exposition early in the composition.

    C. Passacaille (Très large).
       1. The piano presents the theme in the bass. The cello takes it next while the piano plays a single bass line against it. The violin then has the theme while the piano adds a fuller harmonic support. This complete process is repeated with still more voices until the climax is reached over a pedal point in the piano. There is a gradual reduction of parts to the end.

    D. Finale.
       1. The entire movement is built on three thematic ideas which have closely associated rhythms.
       2. The movement opens in a fast 5/4 with a cello tremolo under the arpeggiated harmonics of the violins. The piano gives the first statement of the theme.

BIBLIOGRAPHY

Books

1. Brook, D.   *Five Great French Composers*. London: Rockliff, 1946.
    (ML390 B871f)

2. Demuth, N.   *Ravel*. London: J. M. Dent, 1947. (ML410 R25D38)

3. Goss, M. B.   *Boléro, the Life of Maurice Ravel*. New York: Henry Holt, 1940. (ML410 R25G67)

4. Manuel, R.   *Maurice Ravel*. Trans. by C. Jolly. London: Dobson, 1947.
    (ML410 R25M29J)

5. Miller, H. A.   <u>New Harmonic Devices</u>. Boston: Oliver Ditson Co., 1930.

6. Onnen, F.   <u>Maurice Ravel</u>. Stockholm: Continental Book Co., 194-.
   (ML410 R25058)

7. Seroff, V. I.   <u>Maurice Ravel</u>. New York: Henry Holt, 1953. (ML410
   R25S48)

8. Shera, F. H.   <u>Debussy and Ravel</u>. New York: Oxford University Press,
   1927. (MT92 D28S55)

Periodicals

1. Brian, H.   "Maurice Ravel," <u>MusOp</u> (Nov., 1939)

2. Calvocoressi. M.D.   "When Ravel Composed to Order," <u>ML</u> 22 (1941), 54.

3. Calvocoressi, M.D.   "Maurice Ravel," <u>MT</u> 89 (1938), 22.

4. Casella, A.   "Ravel's Harmony," <u>MT</u> 67 (1926), 124.

5. Cushing, C. C.   "Maurice Ravel: 1875-1937," <u>MM</u> 15 (1938), 140.

6. Hammond, R.   "Maurice Ravel, 1927," <u>MM</u> 5 (1928), 20.

7. Hill, E. B.   "Maurice Ravel," <u>MQ</u> 13 (1927), 130.

8. Landormy, P.   "Maurice Ravel," <u>MQ</u> 25 (1939), 430.

9. Lockspeiser, E.   "Roussel and Ravel," <u>ML</u> 19 (1938), 245.

10. Morris, R. O.   "Maurice Ravel," <u>ML</u> 2 (1921), 274.

11. Ravel, M.   "What I Think of Modern Music," <u>Etude</u> 51 (1933), 571.

12. <u>Revue Musicale, La</u>. April, 1925; December, 1938; entire issues of Jan.,
    Feb., 1939. Appendix to previous issue; all in French.

13. Sabaneev, L.   "Maurice Ravel," <u>MusOp</u> (Aug., 1938).

Music

1. <u>String Quartet in F major</u>. Miniature score and separate parts. New York:
   International Music Co., 1942. (M452 R252.11)

2. <u>Trio in A minor for Violin, Cello, and Piano</u>. Score and separate parts.
   New York: International Music Co., 1944. (M312 R252I)

3. <u>Introduction et allegro</u> . . . (Harp septet). Score and separate parts.
   Paris: Durand, 1906. (M782 R25I)

Maurice Ravel (1875 - 1937)

Records

Title	Music	Recording	Call No.
1. String Quartet (F)		Col 2202 (Juilliard) CH 1123 (Pascal) Col 4668 (Budapest) Phil 104 (Stuyvesant) Mer 10105 (Fine Arts) Vic 146 (Paganini)	
2. Piano Trio (a) (piano, violin, cello)		Vic 1119 (Rubinstein, Heifetz, Piatigorsky) All 3029 (Alma) Mer 10089 (Albeneri)	
3. Introduction and Allegro (harp, flute, clarinet, string quartet)		Cap 8154 (Stockton, Gleghorn, Lurie, Hollywood) Lond 621 (Berghout, Amsterdam) Mer 15006 (La Scala) Strad 1007 (Vito, Eidus, Stradivarius)	

Date Due

NOV 27 '63			